HOPE

Pathways to a Brighter Future

By

ELIJAH M. JAMES, Ph.D.

Copyright © 2024
All rights reserved

No part of this book may be reproduced in any form or by any electronic or mechanical means, without permission in writing from the publisher.

Canadian Cataloguing in Publication Data
James, Elijah M.
Hope: Pathways to a Brighter Future

ISBN 978-1-7383576-0-4

EJ Publishing
White Hills Run
Hammonds Plains
Nova Scotia, Canada B4B 1W7

This book is dedicated to the memory of my cousin, Samuel James who fought the good fight, finished the race, and kept the faith. Henceforth there is laid up for him the crown of righteousness, which the Lord, the righteous judge, will award to him on that Day, and not only to him but also to all who have loved His appearing.

Contents

Preface 11
Acknowledgements 13

CHAPTER 1: THE MEANING AND SIGNIFICANCE OF HOPE 15
    Hope Defined 16
    Sayings about Hope 17
    The Bible on Hope 20
    The Role of Hope in Human Existence 22
    Prayer 24

CHAPTER 2: THE SOURCE OF HOPE 25
    Realistic Reasons for Hope 26
    Prayer 31

CHAPTER 3: VICTORY OVER SIN 32
    What is Sin? 32
    The Consequences of Sin 34
    Hope for Victory over Sin 40
    Prayer 41

CHAPTER 4: THOSE WHO HAVE HOPE 42
    Characteristics of the Hopeful 42
    The Importance of Hope 45
    False Hope 47
    Bible Verses on False Hope 50
    Overcoming False Hope 51

    The ACD Technique 51

    Prayer... 52

CHAPTER 5: SALVATION AND HOPE 53

    Definition of Salvation 53

    Who Needs Salvation? 57

    The Cost of Salvation... 58

    Free but not Cheap.. 58

    Steps to Salvation... 59

    What Must I Do to Be Saved? 61

    Hope of Salvation 62

    Prayer... 62

CHAPTER 6: REDEMPTION... 66

    Definition of Redemption 67

    The Relationship between Salvation and Redemption 67

    The Bible on Redemption... 69

    Sayings about Redemption 71

    The Story of Redemption 74

    Hope and Redemption 76

    Redeemed... 77

    Prayer... 80

CHAPTER 7: FAITH AND HOPE **82**

    Faith Defined.. 82

    Degrees of Faith 82

    Sayings about Faith 83

    The Bible on Faith 85

Faith's Hall of Fame 85
Bible Verses about Faith 89
The Importance of Faith in Our Lives 91
Relationship between Faith and Hope........................... 93
Prayer... 95

CHAPTER 8: PRAYER... 97
What is Prayer? 97
Sayings about Prayer... 97
The Bible on Prayer 101
The Model Prayer.. 104
Notable Pray-ers and Their Prayers in the Bible.......... 105
The Power of Prayer 113
Hope and Prayer 115
Prayer.. 115

CHAPTER 9: WISDOM 116
What is Wisdom?... 117
Wisdom versus Knowledge... 117
Sayings about Wisdom 118
The Bible on Wisdom... 122
The Benefits of Wisdom 126
Benefits of Wisdom to the Individual 126
Hope and Wisdom 129
Two Poems about Wisdom 129
Prayer.. 133

CHAPTER 10: HOPE AND RACISM 134
    Definition of Racism 135
    Does Racism Still Exist? 135
    The Bible on Racism 138
    The Effects of Racism on Society 139
    The Effects of Racism on the Individual 139
    How to Develop Racial Harmony 140
    Hope and Racism 141
    Prayer 142

CHAPTER 11: SATAN AND HOPE 143
    Satan 144
    Other Names for Satan 145
    Satan's Army 148
    Satan's Objectives and Strategies 149
    Satan's Ultimate Goal 149
    The Outcome of the Cosmic Conflict 153
    Hope and the Cosmic Conflict 153
    Prayer 154

CHAPTER 12: BAPTISM 155
    The Definition of Baptism 156
    Baptism versus Christening 156
    The Significance of Baptism 156
    Bible Verses about Baptism 157
    Special Note 159
    Sayings about Baptism 159
    Who Should Perform Baptisms 164

Baptism and Hope 165
Prayer 166

CHAPTER 13: THE TRINITY 167
The Trinity in the Bible 168
God the Father 173
God the Son 173
God the Holy Spirit 174
Hope and the Trinity 175
Prayer 176

CHAPTER 14: ANGELS 177
What are Angels 178
Bible Verses about Angels 178
Types or Categories of Angels 181
The Nature of Angels 187
Quotes about Angels 189
Hope and Angels 191
Poem 192
Prayer 193

CHAPTER 15: THE STATE OF THE DEAD 194
Where Are the Dead? 195
Body, Spirit, and Soul 196
The Death of the Soul 197
Spirit and Body Re-united 198
Hope and the Resurrection 200
Prayer 200

CHAPTER 16: CRIME 201
    What is Crime? 201
    Types of Crimes 202
    Sayings about Crimes 203
    The Bible on Crime 205
    The Benefits and Costs of Crime 207
    Reasons for Crime 211
    Back to the Bible 213
    A Few Tips on Crime Prevention 214
    Hope and Crime 216
    Prayer 217

CHAPTER 17: HELL 218
    What is Hell? 219
    Hell is Real 219
    Sayings about Hell 220
    Bible Verses about Hell 222
    The Impact of a Belief in Hell 224
    The Purpose of Hell 225
    Hope and Hell 226
    Prayer 227

CHAPTER 18: GRACE 228
    Introduction 228
    Grace Defined 229
    Sayings about Grace 229
    The Bible on Grace 232

    The Significance of Grace 236

    Marvelous Grace.. 238

    Amazing Grace 239

    Hope and Grace... 239

    Prayer... 240

CHAPTER 19: THE NEW EARTH 241

    The Earth God Created 241

    The Cursed Earth 242

    Vacation in Heaven... 243

    Millennium on Earth 246

    The Earth Made New 247

    The Pearly White City 248

    Hope and the New Earth... 249

    Prayer... 249

CLOSING REMARKS 250

Preface

The world is in turmoil. The breakdown of law and order in Haiti, Climate change, racism, wars, hunger, injustice, gender inequality, and communicable diseases such as AIDS and COVID-19 are just some of the critical issues that occupy the minds of millions of people today. Millions are frustrated and millions more don't know which way to turn. In a world like ours, often overshadowed by uncertainty and adversity, we need uplifting; we need inspiration and motivation; we need optimistic expectations. In a word, we need *Hope*.

Hope: Pathways to a Brighter Future stands as a testament to the enduring power of hope offering a sanctuary of solace and encouragement for those seeking consolation and strength to persevere. The book is organized into 19 chapters covering diverse topics such as Victory over Sin, Faith and Hope, Hope and Racism, Salvation and Hope, and controversial theological questions such as the State of the Dead and the Trinity. It empowers us to imagine a brighter future, to envision possibilities beyond the realm of what is presently known, and to take bold steps toward manifesting those aspirations.

However, this book does not pretend to be a proverbial *balm in Gilead* that banishes all hardships or guarantees a life devoid of struggle. Rather, it acknowledges the reality of human existence and embraces the complexities that accompany our search for a better life. It acknowledges that hope, at times, may seem elusive, that it may be tested and strained, and that it may require courage, patience, and resilience to sustain.

Pathways to a Brighter Future

As you delve into the chapters that lie ahead, may you discover the strength to confront your own trials, the wisdom to navigate the turbulent waters of uncertainty, and the resilience to hold onto hope when the world feels unforgiving. May this book become a companion on your journey, reminding you of the vast wellspring of hope that resides within you, waiting to be tapped into and nurtured.

Together, let us embark on this journey that acknowledges the shadows but forever remains anchored in the light. Let us remember that it is through hope that we find the courage to envision a better world, to create a legacy of compassion and understanding, and to forge a path toward a future that transcends the boundaries of our imagination.

May *Hope: Pathways to a Brighter Future* serve as a source of inspiration, guidance, and affirmation, reminding us that even amidst the harshest storms, hope endures. With hope as our guiding light, let us embark on this transformative journey together.

Acknowledgements

A work of this nature is often the result of contributions from several sources. This is no exception. I would like to express my heartfelt gratitude to all those who have contributed in one way or another to the completion of this book. Without your input, this project would not have been possible.

First and foremost, I extend my deepest appreciation to my dear friend and colleague, Miss Koren Norton, for her invaluable insights and knowledge. Koren, your unwavering commitment and dedication to my well-being have been instrumental in the writing of this book. I owe you a tremendous debt of gratitude for the sacrifices you have made. Thanks for your generous help.

I have benefited immensely from discussions with the members of the Elders' Quartet in Montreal, Canada, on many of the topics in this book. Alfred Meade and Byron St. Clair will recognize their views on many issues in this book. The late Ezra Clarke will be greatly missed. I thank you all. Ezra knew all along that there was singing up in heaven.

I credit the completion of this book in large part to the fervent prayers of many friends including Rev. Carlwin Greenaway, Mrs. Karen St. Rose, Father Joel St. Rose, Mrs. Inez Stevens, and Mrs. Juliett Sheppard. I thank you sincerely for your prayers and your constant support and encouragement.

I am indebted to the numerous individuals who generously shared their knowledge, experiences, and ideas with me. Your willingness to open up and provide me with the necessary information has enriched this book and added depth to its content. I would also like to extend my gratitude to the research institutions, libraries, and archives that provided access to valuable resources, enabling me to gather the information needed to bring this book to life.

The images at the beginning of each chapter are taken from Microsoft Word Online Pictures. I am truly thankful for that very helpful feature.

I am immensely grateful to the publishing team at EJ Publishing. Thank you for believing in this project and for your meticulous attention to detail in editing, designing, and promoting the book. Your expertise has transformed a rough manuscript into a beautiful book. Thank you all for being a part of this incredible journey. Your contributions have made this book a reality, and I am forever grateful.

Sincerely,

Elijah M. James

CHAPTER 1: THE MEANING AND SIGNIFICANCE OF HOPE

The dove is often used as a symbol for hope.

For I know the plans I have for you, declares the Lord, plans to prosper you and not to harm you, plans to give you hope and a future (Jeremiah 29:11).

What is this thing called hope? And why is it so important that anyone would want to write about it? In this introductory chapter, we explore the meaning of hope by looking at it from different perspectives. We also share with you some important quotations about hope so that you can get a glimpse into how others view hope. A discussion of the role of hope in human existence ends this introductory chapter.

Hope Defined

As a noun, hope can be defined as a state of optimism originating from the expectation that some desired outcome will materialize. Thus, one can entertain the hope of success in an upcoming tournament. As a verb, to hope is to expect confidently and with anticipation. For example, "We hope that the flight arrives on time."

Note that one does not hope that something will happen if the event has already occurred. It would border on irrationality or perhaps even insanity if one were to hope to win a lottery that has already been won. Notice that the terms "expectation" and "anticipation" in the definition are future-oriented.

One useful way to envision hope is to look at its opposite. The opposite of hope is despair. The Oxford Dictionary defines despair as "the complete loss or absence of hope." Hope is bright, despair is dark. Hope sees a future to be desired, despair says it's the end. Hope engages in planning, despair asks, What is the point? Hope continues the struggle, despair throws in the towel.

Sayings about Hope

   We have provided a clear definition of hope so that we can identify it. Let us now see what others have said about hope in order to get an even clearer picture of hope. I have selected 25 sayings about hope. As we read these sayings, let us reflect deeply on what they really mean.

1. "Optimism is the faith that leads to achievement. Nothing can be done without hope and confidence." – **Helen Keller**

2. "You are not here merely to make a living, you are here in order to enable the world to live more amply, with greater vision, with a finer spirit of hope and achievement. You are here to enrich the world, and you impoverish yourself if you forget the errand." – **Woodrow Wilson**

3. "We must accept finite disappointment, but never lose infinite hope." – **Martin Luther King, Jr.**

4. "All kids need is a little help, a little hope and somebody who believes in them." – **Magic Johnson**

5. "It's always something, to know you've done the most you could. But, don't leave off hoping, or it's of no use doing anything. Hope, hope to the last." – **Charles Dickens**

6. "We must vote for hope, vote for life, vote for a brighter future for all of our loved ones." – **Ed Markey**

7. "Hope is the companion of power, and mother of success; for who so hopes strongly has within him the gift of miracles." – **Samuel Smiles**

Pathways to a Brighter Future

8. "A dream is the bearer of a new possibility, the enlarged horizon, the great hope." – **Howard Thurman**

9. "We have always held to the hope, the belief, the conviction that there is a better life, a better world, beyond the horizon." – **Franklin D. Roosevelt**

10. "Learn from yesterday, live for today, hope for tomorrow. The important thing is not to stop questioning." – **Albert Einstein**

11. "Hope is important because it can make the present moment less difficult to bear. If we believe that tomorrow will be better, we can bear a hardship today." – **Thich Nhat Hanh**

12. "Our human compassion binds us the one to the other – not in pity or patronizingly, but as human beings who have learnt how to turn our common suffering into hope for the future." – **Nelson Mandela**

13. "Hope smiles from the threshold of the year to come, whispering 'it will be happier'…" – **Alfred Lord Tennyson**

14. "In fact, hope is best gained after defeat and failure, because then inner strength and toughness is produced." – **Fritz Knapp**

15. "A positive statement propels hope toward a better future, it builds up your faith and that of others, and it promotes change." – **Jan Dargatz**

16. "Hope is being able to see that there is light despite all of the darkness." – **Desmond Tutu**

HOPE

17. "There was never a night or a problem that could defeat sunrise or hope." – **Bernard Williams**

18. "Let your hopes, not your hurts, shape your future." – **Robert H. Schuller**

19. "I think it's a mistake to ever look for hope outside of one's self." – **Arthur Miller**

20. "Hope is the only bee that makes honey without flowers." – **Robert Green Ingersoll**

21. "Hope fills the holes of my frustration in my heart." – **Emanuel Cleaver**

22. "Time is no longer endless or the horizon destitute of hope." – **Charles Lindbergh**

23. "A whole stack of memories never equal one little hope." – **Charles M. Schulz**

24. "He who has health, has hope; and he who has hope has everything." – **Thomas Carlyle**

25. "To live without hope is to cease to live." – **Fyodor Dostoyevsky**

Source: https://www.shutterfly.com/ideas/hope-quotes/#Famous%20Quotes%20About%20Hope

Pathways to a Brighter Future

The Bible on Hope

Not surprisingly, the Bible is not silent on hope. Along with Faith and Love, it is one of the principles of Christian living. In this section, we quote 20 Bible verses about hope that will cheer us up along the way and brighten our path.

1. Therefore my heart is glad, and my glory rejoices; my flesh also will rest in hope. **(Psalm 16:9)**

2. You are my hiding place and my shield; I hope in Your word. **(Psalm 119:14)**

3. O Israel, hope in the LORD; for with the LORD there is mercy, and with Him is abundant redemption. **(Psalm 130:7)**

4. The LORD takes pleasure in those who fear Him, in those who hope in His mercy. **(Psalm 147:11)**

5. For surely there is a hereafter, and your hope will not be cut off. **(Proverbs 23:18)**

6. Blessed is the man who trusts in the LORD, and whose hope is the LORD. **(Jeremiah 17:7)**

7. For I know the thoughts that I think toward you, says the LORD, thoughts of peace and not of evil, to give you a future and a hope. **(Jeremiah 29:11)**

8. 'The LORD is my portion,' says my soul, 'therefore I hope in Him!' **(Lamentations 3:24)**

9. Now hope does not disappoint, because the love of God has been poured out in our hearts by the Holy Spirit [which] was given to us. **(Romans 5:5)**

HOPE

10. Rejoicing in hope, patient in tribulation, continuing steadfastly in prayer." **(Romans 12:12)**

11. For whatever things were written before were written for our learning, that we through the patience and comfort of the Scriptures might have hope. **(Romans 15:4)**

12. Now may the God of hope fill you with all joy and peace in believing, that you may abound in hope by the power of the Holy Spirit. **(Romans 15:13)**

13. The eyes of your understanding being enlightened; that you may know what is the hope of His calling, what are the riches of the glory of His inheritance in the saints. **(Ephesians 1:18)**

14. To them God willed to make known what are the riches of the glory of this mystery among the Gentiles: which is Christ in you, the hope of glory." **(Colossians 1:27)**

15. We remember before our God and Father your work produced by faith, your labor prompted by love, and your endurance inspired by hope in our Lord Jesus Christ. **(1 Thessalonians 1:3)**

16. But let us who are of the day be sober, putting on the breastplate of faith and love, and as a helmet the hope of salvation. **(1 Thessalonians 5:8)**

17. In hope of eternal life which God, who cannot lie, promised before time began. **(Titus 1:2)**

18. Looking for the blessed hope and glorious appearing of our great God and Savior Jesus Christ. **(Titus 2:13)**

19. Let us hold unswervingly to the hope we profess, for he who promised is faithful. **(Hebrews 10:23)**

20. And everyone who has this hope in Him purifies himself, just as He is pure. **(1 John 3:3)**

Source: https://lifehopeandtruth.com/bible/bible-study/encouraging-bible-verses/encouraging-bible-verses-about-hope/#:~:text=Hopeful%20Bible%20Verses&text=%E2%80%9CTherefore%20my%20heart%20is%20glad,also%20will%20rest%20in%20hope.%E2%80%9D&text=%E2%80%9CYou%20are%20my%20hiding%20place,I%20hope%20in%20Your%20word.%E2%80%9D&text=%E2%80%9CO%20Israel%2C%20hope%20in%20the,with%20Him%20is%20abundant%20redemption.%E2%80%9D

The Role of Hope in Human Existence

One of the best ways to conceptualize the role of hope is to imagine your life with all the things you hope for—to successfully launch your career, to complete your degree, to start a business, to go on a cruise, to meet the man/woman of your dreams, fall in love, and get married, to raise a family, etc., etc. Exciting, eh? You have a reason or reasons for living and life is worth living. *You* are a hopeful person.

Now, imagine your life with not even a shred of hope—no prospects for a job, nothing positive in the future, only doom and gloom. There is no light at the end of the tunnel. You can't think of a reason for living, and it seems as if the world will be better without you. Such is the state of a hopeless person. But you don't have to be hopeless. Regardless of your present circumstances, you can find hope in Christ who died so that you can live in hope.

HOPE

The story is told of a man who was thrown into the depths of despair. Deciding to end his life, he climbed into a tree with the intent to jump to his death after he ate his last meal, a banana. He ate his banana, but before he jumped, he looked down and saw another man eating the banana pealing that he had discarded. He then realized that there was someone who was worse off than he was. He figured that there was hope for him after all. He decided to live. Hope changed his outlook on life.

The following statement about hope could hardly be more apt.

Hope

"If you only carry one thing throughout your life, let it be hope. Let it be hope that better things are always ahead. Let it be hope that you can get through even the toughest times. Let it be hope that you are stronger than any challenge that comes your way. Let it be hope that you are exactly where you are meant to be right now, and that you are on the path to where you are meant to be… Because during these times, hope will be the very thing that carries you through." **Nikki Banas**

May the God of heaven, in whom we believe, fill us with hope in Him as we travel through life's hills and valleys, knowing that He is with us and will never leave us.

Prayer

Our Father in Heaven, we come to you this moment recognizing that You are all-powerful. We pray that You will grant us hope as we travel through life's journey. Give us hope, Father, so that we can navigate life's meandering streams with optimism.

Amen.

CHAPTER 2: THE SOURCE OF HOPE

God is the source of hope. His word gives us hope.

I pray that God, the source of hope, will fill you completely with joy and peace because you trust in him. Then you will overflow with confident hope through the power of the Holy Spirit (Romans 15:13).

Notice that the singular "source" rather than the plural "sources" is used as the title of the chapter. The point being made is that there is only one main source of hope, and that is God. There may be myriads of reasons for hope as we shall soon see, but there is only one person from whom hope originates.

Realistic Reasons for Hope

Close family members gathered at the bedside of a lady (let's call her Veron) waiting for her passing as the doctors had assured them that it was just a matter of minutes before she would pass. Veron was still alive several hours after, and one of the nurses wondered what was keeping her alive. She asked whether Veron was expecting anyone else to come to see her, and was told that her son was expected. The nurse explained that Veron was probably waiting for her son to arrive. The son arrived, went to Veron, touched her, and said, "Mom, I am here." Veron opened her eyes, looked at her son, closed her eyes again, and died peacefully shortly thereafter.

Hope kept Veron alive until her son arrived. It was the hope of seeing his mother alive that helped her son endure the hardships of the journey. Hope is, indeed, a powerful motivator. Here are some realistic reasons for hope.

1. God loves us

For God so loved the world that he gave his one and only Son, that whoever believes in him shall not perish but have eternal life. **(John 3:16)**

When you are bombarded on every side, when you are thrown into the abyss of despair, when the storms of life toss you to and fro, when your best friend betrays you, when your life feels empty and worthless, when everyone seems to hate you, remember that the Almighty God loves you. Not only that, but He gave His only Son so that you can have everlasting life. Yes, God loves you

HOPE

and me, and that's reason for hope. The songwriter Frederick Martin Lehman writes:

The love of God is greater far
Than tongue or pen can ever tell;
It goes beyond the highest star,
And reaches to the lowest hell;

2. God will never leave us

Fear not, for I am with you; be not dismayed, for I am your God; I will strengthen you, I will help you, I will uphold you with my righteous right hand. **(Isaiah 41:10)**

When thou passest through the waters, I will be with thee; and through the rivers, they shall not overflow thee: when thou walkest through the fire, thou shalt not be burned; neither shall the flame kindle upon thee. **(Isaiah 43:2)**

These verses from scripture assure us that God is always with us. Through the fires of stormy relationships, through the rough waters of broken hearts, and through the rivers of bereavement, God promises that He will always be with us. His promises are sure. We can be confident in His word because He cannot lie.

3. God is omniscient

For whenever our heart condemns us, God is greater than our heart, and he knows everything. (**1 John 3:20**)

Sometimes, all we need is for someone to understand us, our concerns, and our predicament. Often, we don't even require any action on anybody's part. Well, we can take comfort and have hope knowing that God knows everything.

4. God cares

You have taken account of my miseries; Put my tears in your bottle. Are they not in your book? **(Psalm 56:8)**.

The psalmist was quite confident that God cared, and we can be just as confident that He cares for you and me. He cares so much for us that *"He will order his angels to protect you wherever you go"* **(Psalm 91:11).**

The following popular song provides assurance that God does care.

Does Jesus care when my heart is pained
Too deeply for mirth and song?
When the burdens press
And the cares distress
And the way grows weary and long?

Oh, yes, He cares, I know He cares
His heart is touched with my grief
When the days are weary
The long night dreary
I know my Savior cares

Does Jesus care when my way is dark
With a nameless dread and fear?
And as the daylight fades
Into deep dark shades
Does He care enough to be near?

Does Jesus care
When I've tried and failed
To resist some temptation strong?

When for my deep grief there's no relief
Though the tears flow all the day long

Does Jesus care when I've said, "Goodbye"
To the dearest on earth to me
And my sad heart aches
Till it nearly breaks
Is it aught to Him? Does He see?

(J. Lincoln Hall & Frank E. Graeff)

5. God is loyal and faithful

Let us hold unswervingly to the hope we profess, for he who promised is faithful. (**Hebrews 10:23**).

Broken promises, betrayal of trust, and misplaced confidence are all too familiar experiences for many of us. And some of these disappointments can have disastrous consequences. God's loyalty and faithfulness are certain and unchanging. This is a tremendous reason for hope.

6. God is good, and whatever He does is good

Oh, taste and see that the Lord is good! Blessed is the man who takes refuge in him! (**Psalm 34:8**).

The knowledge that God is good always is another realistic reason for hope. Evidence of God's goodness can be seen in the falling rain that waters the thirsty earth, in the rising of the sun that brightens the day, in the flowers that bloom, in the birds that sing, and in the beauty of the flowing rivers. Psalm 145:17 tells us that whatever God does is good. Even in our darkest moments, we can find hope in that fact. Surely, we can join the psalmist in declaring that, "Everything God does is perfect." **(Psalm 18:30)**

7. God is in control

That people may know, from the rising of the sun and from the west, that there is none besides me; I am the Lord, and there is no other. I form light and create darkness, I make well-being and create calamity, I am the Lord, who does all these things. **(Isaiah 45:6-7)**

In good times and in bad times, in times of abundance and in times of scarcity, in gladness and in sadness, in wealth and in poverty, in pleasure and in pain, just know that the King of kings and the Lord of lords is always in full control. When you ponder over the difficult theological question, "Why do bad things happen to good people?", be of good cheer, and take courage, God is in control. And whatever He does is good.

The following poem by La'shawna Howard encapsulates the idea that God is in full control.

God is in Control

No matter what you have been told
God is in control
Yes, they came with a report one day
But God has the last say
Rest assured he is near
No need to fear

Hold on to Faith real tight
Know that everything is going to be all right
When God is in the midst
Defeat doesn't exist

HOPE

You serve a God who can make a bird sing a beautiful melody
A God who can calm the sea
A God who holds your destiny
He is your healing spring
And in his hands he brings

Hope
Strength
Life
Love
Newness
and Joy

All just for you, because his love is everlasting and true

Source: https://www.familyfriendpoems.com/poem/god-is-in-control

Prayer

    Holy Father in heaven, the one from whom all blessings flow, we bow humbly before your presence to thank You for revealing to us that You are the source of hope. Help us, dear Father, to place our trust in You, knowing that you love us with an everlasting love. We pray in the name of Jesus, our Lord and Saviour.

    Amen

Pathways to a Brighter Future

CHAPTER 3: VICTORY OVER SIN

Through the sacrificial death of Jesus Christ on the cross, we can gain victory over sin.

But God is the One Who gives us power over sin through Jesus Christ our Lord. We give thanks to Him for this (1 Corinthians 15:57).

What is Sin?

Whosoever committeth sin transgresseth also the law, for sin is the transgression of the law. **(1 John 3:4).**

Here we have a simple, straightforward, uncomplicated definition of sin. It is any act that violates God's laws outlined in the Ten Commandments and listed below:

1. You shall have no other Gods before me.

2. Thou shalt not make unto thee any graven images.

3. Thou shalt not take the name of the Lord thy God in vain.

4. Remember the Sabbath day and keep it Holy.

5. Honor your father and mother.

6. Thou shalt not kill.

7. Thou shalt not commit adultery.

8. Thou shalt not steal.

9. Thou shall not bear false witness.

10. You shall not covet.

(Exodus 20: 2-17)

These commandments are repeated in Deuteronomy 5: 6-21.

When we violate any of these laws, we commit sin. When we bear false witness (lie), steal, dishonor our parents, commit murder or transgress any of God's laws, someone gets hurt or is adversely affected. Ultimately, sin hurts God. When we break God's laws, we sin against Him. Joseph refused to succumb to Potiphar's wife, saying, *"There is none greater in this house than I, neither hath he kept back anything from me but thee, because thou art his wife. How then can I do this great wickedness, and sin against God?"* **(Genesis 39:9)**.

Similarly, when King David coveted Uriah's wife, Bathsheba, and had him killed, he said, *"Against you, you only, have I sinned and done what is evil in your sight."* **(Psalm 51:4)**.

The Consequences of Sin

Sin has some serious consequences, including:

- Separation from God

- Devaluation of self-worth

- Enslavement

- Enmity with God

- Diseases

- Curses

- Poverty

- Death

We will discuss each of these in turn.

Sin Separates the Sinner from God

But your iniquities have separated you from your God (Isaiah 59:2)

It should not be too difficult to explain why sin separates the sinner from God. When you break the law, you end up on the wrong side of the law. When you violate God's laws, you go against God, and that means you separate yourself from Him. Sin breaks the relationship with God and that means you are separated from Him. Does that mean the relationship cannot be fixed? Certainly not! You can renew your relationship with God by repenting. Yes, if we genuinely go to God, tell Him we are sorry, and ask His forgiveness, He will welcome us back with open arms. "If we confess our sins, he is faithful and just and will forgive us our sins and purify us from all unrighteousness." (1 John 1:9)

However, we must be careful not to be presumptuous and sin just because we know that God will forgive us. If we sin unintentionally, as we often do, we confess, acknowledge the error of our ways, ask for forgiveness, and try not to repeat the transgression. When we sin presumptuously, it's intentional and tends to be repetitive. As long as we persist in the sin, it's a sign that repentance has not occurred, and if we have not repented, God will not forgive us. We remain separated from God.

Sin Devalues Human Beings

When God created human beings, he created them with dignity and power. They were valuable. Witness the story in Genesis. Then God said, "And now we will make human beings; they will be like us and resemble us. They will have power over the fish, the birds, and all animals, domestic and wild, large and small." So God created human beings, making them to be like himself. He created them male and female, blessed them, and said, "Have many children, so that your descendants will live all over the earth and bring it under their control. I am putting you in charge of the fish, the birds, and all the wild animals..." (Genesis 1:26-28). Clearly, they had every reason to have a high sense of self-worth.

Furthermore, the psalmist declared:

"What is mankind that you are mindful of them, human beings that you care for them? You have made them a little lower than the angels and crowned them with glory and honor. You made them rulers over the works of your hands; you put everything under their feet." (Psalm 8:4-6).

Satan tries to rob you of the glory and honor that God bestowed upon you by trying to get you to transgress the laws of God. We have all sinned (Romans 3:23), but if we confess, repent, and ask for forgiveness, God is faithful and just to forgive us. He will restore us to our former state.

Sin Enslaves the Sinner

Slavery is not just a loss of freedom; it is a denial of one's identity. When we develop a sinful nature, it becomes difficult to give up sin; and the more we indulge in sin, the easier it is to continue in sin. In that way, we become slaves to sin. We are in bondage, and we surrender our identities as followers of Christ. No wonder the apostle Paul makes mention of the sin that so easily entangles us. Once you are living a life of sin, you are a captive of Satan whose objective is to steal, kill and destroy. (John 10:10). However, God has provided a way of escape through Jesus Christ. We can escape the clutches of sin by the process of repentance which involves being sorry for transgressing God's laws, asking for forgiveness, and turning away from sin. We can regain our identity.

Sin Causes Enmity with God

Not only does sin separate the sinner from God, but it also makes the sinner an enemy of God and a friend of Satan. An enemy (adversary) of God is one who fights against God, opposes His will, and seeks to do Him harm. Obviously, Satan is at enmity with God. 1 Timothy 5:14-15 makes this abundantly clear, and sinners join Satan's forces against God. As the chief enemy of God, Satan is on a mission to alienate us from God, and his maim ammunition is to tempt us to break God's commandments. Sin makes us enemies of God, but Jesus restores us. Witness this verse:

You are my friends if you do what I command. (John 15:14)

Isn't that good news? No more enemies of God, but friends, if we keep His commandments.

Sin Causes Diseases

He said, *"If you listen carefully to the Lord your God and do what is right in his eyes, if you pay attention to his commands and keep all his decrees, I will not bring on you any of the diseases I brought on the Egyptians, for I am the Lord, who heals you."* (Exodus 15:26)

This passage of scripture does not say that every illness or disease is caused by sin, but it does say that refraining from sin will prevent the onset of certain diseases. Stealing, lying, covetousness, and other sins may leave the perpetrator feeling guilty and anxious which may result in some form of mental illness. The mind and body are closely connected, so when there is a disorder in the mind, the body will be adversely affected. For example, if a mental illness prevents you from eating, the body will become weak and susceptible to diseases and illnesses.

Sin Causes Curses

A curse is a pronouncement of harm, evil, or misfortune on someone or something. In the same way that obeying God's commandments brings blessings, so too, disobeying them causes curses. Pay attention to the following verse:

"But it shall come to pass, if you do not obey the voice of the LORD your God, to observe carefully all His commandments and His statutes which I command you today, that all these curses will come upon you and overtake you." (Deuteronomy 28:15).

When we deliberately and repeatedly break God's commandments, we remove ourselves from his protection and expose ourselves to curses. These curses can be in the form of various misfortunes, financial ruin, diseases, accidents, and other events that cause damage and harm. We can stay protected under the wings of the Almighty. As the songwriter puts it:

"Under His wings, O what precious enjoyment

There will I hide till life's trials are o'er;

Sheltered, protected, no evil can harm me,

Resting in Jesus I'm safe evermore."

(William Cushing)

Sin Causes Poverty

"Whoever loves pleasure will be a poor man; he who loves wine and oil will not be rich.... He who follows worthless pursuits will have plenty of poverty." (Proverbs 21:17; 28:19)

Although this passage of scripture does not tell us that poverty is the direct result of disobeying any specific commandment of God, such as stealing, or telling lies, or murder, it does point out that anyone who follows a worthless lifestyle invites poverty upon himself or herself. People are less likely to be poor if they adopt lifestyles that are healthier and more in compliance with God's ideal. The lifestyle of "riotous living" that was pursued by the prodigal son, led to waste and poverty. (Luke 15:11-32). Laziness and idleness are other traits that can lead to poverty. We too, like the prodigal son, can make a right-about turn, forsake a life of futile living, and enjoy the riches of our heavenly Father.

Sin Causes Death

The story of death and sin in Genesis is well-known. It was disobedience of God's orders that led to death. God ordered the first couple in their Eden home not to eat the fruit of a certain tree. Tempted by Satan, Eve disobeyed God's orders. The consequence was death. "By the sweat of your brow you will eat your food until you return to the ground, since from it you were taken; for dust you are and to dust you will return." (Genesis 3:19). The apostle Paul reminds us that "The wages of sin is death..." (Romans 6:23), and in Ezekiel 18:20 we read, "The soul that sins shall surely die."

Worse than physical death is spiritual death mentioned in Revelation 21:8:

"But the cowardly, the unbelieving, the vile, the murderers, the sexually immoral, those who practice magic arts, the idolaters and all liars-their place will be in the fiery lake of burning sulfur. This is the second death."

We have a choice. We can choose a life of sin which leads to death, or a life with Christ which leads to life eternal.

Hope for Victory over Sin

We have seen the devastating consequences of sin. Those who believe in God live in anticipation, expecting that one day, they will gain victory over sin and Satan. In fact, those who accept Christ as their Saviour, turn away from a life of sin, and are walking in newness of life have already gained the victory over sin. Satan, the enemy, will continue to tempt us; and yes, we may sometimes yield to temptation, but we do not have to. "I can do all things through Christ who strengthens me." (Philippians 4:13). There will be an end to sin, sorrow, pain, and death. This is what the Bible has to say:

"And God shall wipe away all tears from their eyes; and there shall be no more death, neither sorrow, nor crying, neither shall there be any more pain: for the former things are passed away." (Revelation 21:4).

What a glorious day that will be!

HOPE

Prayer

Our Heavenly Father, in whom we live and move, and owe our existence, we understand the devastating nature of sin, and we do not want to be separated from You. We confess our sins to You, and we pray that You will forgive us. We pray that You will help us, through the power of Your Holy Spirit, to be victorious over sin. We pray in Jesus' Name.

CHAPTER 4: THOSE WHO HAVE HOPE

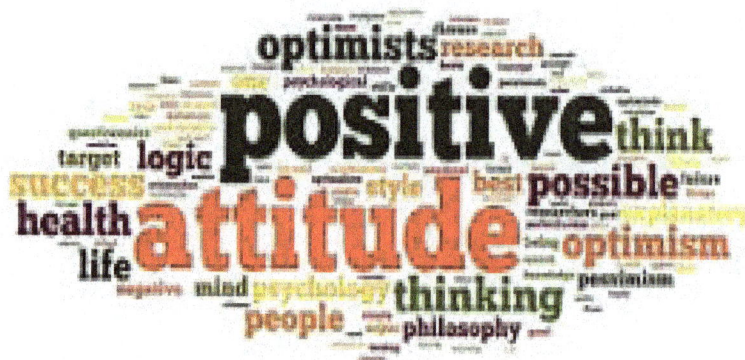

People who have hope are optimistic. They have a positive outlook on life.

"Through him we have also obtained access by faith into this grace in which we stand, and we rejoice in hope of the glory of God" (Romans 5:2).

Characteristics of the Hopeful

A great deal can be said about those who have hope. In this section, we shall discuss some of the characteristics of the hopeful so that those who have a desire to be more hopeful can cultivate some of these characteristics. It must be borne in mind that the presence of any of these characteristics in an individual is not an absolute guarantee that the individual will be hopeful, but it is likely that such an individual will be more hopeful than someone who does not possess any of these traits.

Optimism

Optimism seems to be a trait of hopeful people. They seem to be optimistic about outcomes, about the future, and about everything in general. They are able to cope with difficulties because they see the calm after the storm. Their optimism spills over to others and causes them to be optimistic also. Another point worth noting in this regard is that optimistic people seem to attract optimistic people. "Birds of a feather flock together."

Perseverance

People who are hopeful are persistent. If they don't succeed on the first attempt, they will try again. Perseverance is a trade mark of the hopeful. They believe, like the songwriter:

"You can get it if you really want
You can get it if you really want
You can get it if you really want
But you must try, try and try, try and try
You'll succeed at last." **(Jimmy Cliff)**

Their persistence allows them to achieve established goals.

Cooperation

Hopeful people tend to cooperate easily with others as they see fruit in such cooperation. They see cooperation as a positive means whereby projects can be completed as like-minded people push for positive outcomes.

Failure to succumb to obstacles

Obstacles often lie in the way of accomplishing certain desirable goals. People who have hope do not succumb to such obstacles. Instead, they tend to view such hindrances as opportunities. For example, Rick (a factitious character) failed to get the position for which he applied on the grounds that he did not possess the requisite skills. Instead of being discouraged and bitterly disappointed, Rick saw this as an opportunity to obtain some training that would enable him to acquire the skills that he lacked. Such is the tendency of hopeful people to overcome obstacles.

Ability to endure hardship

You may recall the story of Veron and her son in Chapter 2 of this book. It was hope that enabled her to cling to life until her son arrived, and it was hope that made it possible to defeat the odds and arrived at his mother's bedside while she was yet alive. People with hope have the quality of being able to withstand brutal treatment, injustice, poverty, unfair discrimination, etc. because of the hope of finally overcoming such unfairness, or because of the hope of accomplishing some highly valued goal.

Ability to see light beyond the present darkness

Hope ends with the inability to see light in the future. Where there is no hope, life has little or no meaning. For hopeful people, there is always a bright tomorrow. They see the light at the end of the tunnel. They make meaningful plans and work towards the successful implementation of those plans. Hopeful people press forward even in the face of disappointment and apparent failure.

Problem solvers

Having a desire to move forward into the future, people who have hope tend to be problem-solvers. They have certain targeted goals that they want to accomplish, and when problems arise that impede the attainment of those goals, people with hope tend to find solutions for those problems. Thus, they become adept at problem-solving.

The Importance of Hope

Hope incentivizes us

Lesroy (not his real name) was registered in one section of my economics course at university. On the first day of classes, the 19-year-old man walked straight to the back, took a seat, and within a few minutes, assumed a "wake- me-when-it's-over" position. I called out to him and informed him that I would like to see him in my office. He kept the appointment. I discovered that he had no incentive because he felt he would not be given a fair chance. Once Lesroy was given hope that things could change, he was motivated and became a teacher who volunteered in youth development. He was incentivized by hope.

Hope gives us direction

Without hope, we are like ships without rudders, liable to end up anywhere. Without hope, our lives have no purpose, no direction, and no established goals. The proverb 'nothing ventured, nothing gained' applies to those without hope. Whereas we are aimless without hope, the slightest ray of hope transforms us from rudderless vessels to individuals with targeted aims and objectives.

Hope makes us relevant

People who have lost hope tend to feel worthless and that they don't matter. They believe that if they did not exist, it would not matter anywhere. They would not be missed. On the other hand, people who have hope know that they have a mission to accomplish, and a destiny to fulfil. Hope gives them a feeling of usefulness and relevance.

Hope inspires action

Hope gives us something to look forward to, and more often than not, it requires specific action on our part. You hope for a job, apply for it. You hope for a university degree, study the relevant subjects and pass the exams. You hope to own your home within five years, then save towards it. Hope is not just wishful thinking. It involves the desire to take the steps necessary to achieve the thing that is hoped for. Indeed, you may not be able to do anything that may have an impact on the thing that is hoped for, but where possible, hope will inspire action.

Hope gives inner strength

There are numerous real-world instances where hope has enabled people to overcome both physical and mental challenges. Mental illnesses such as depression, anxiety, eating disorders, mental disorders caused by stress, and others have been overcome by hope. The same is true of some physical illnesses such as headaches, and stomach pains. Hope seems to give people the inner strength not only to cope with such illnesses but also to overcome them. They attend counseling sessions, keep medical appointments, and take prescribed medication because of the hope of recovery.

Hope makes life meaningful

One's view of the meaning of life is fashioned significantly by one's view of the future. If the future is viewed with optimism and happiness, life will be seen as meaningful. If the future is bleak, then life will not have much meaning. Life has meaning to hopeful people because they view the future with optimism.

False Hope

Up to this point in this chapter, we have discussed certain characteristics of the hopeful and the importance of hope. In this section, we will explore the concept of false hope and its dangers.

Definition of False Hope

Hope, as we have seen earlier, is a confident expectation that a desired event will happen. Of course, there is such a thing as false hope. The leader of a hiking group announced that one destination was only about 15 minutes away, thus arousing the hope that the next longed-for break would be in 15 minutes. In fact, the destination was just over 20 minutes away. The hikers' hope, in this instance, was false. We can define false hope as follows:

False hope is the emotion of confidence that something will happen when, in fact, it will not.

It is the anticipation of an unrealizable event. It should be noted that false hope is not hopelessness. It is not the absence of hope. It is not despair.

Dangers of False Hope

False hope can lead to several negative consequences, including the following:

Discouragement

At least some members of the hiking expedition referred to above would likely be discouraged or disappointed when, after the anticipated 15 minutes, there was no destination in sight. Some members could have dug deep into their energy reserves to eke out 15 minutes of hiking; hope now morphed into discouragement and disappointment.

Despair

When you exert all your effort into building up confidence that a certain event will happen only to find out that the event will never materialize, the result is likely to be hopelessness. Not only will you despair that the particular event will happen, but you will tend to lose hope that other things hoped for will not happen.

Unrealistic worldview

We live in a world with limitations. This suggests that we should entertain realistic hopes. If we consistently entertain unrealistic hopes, we will tend to cultivate an unrealistic worldview. This will tend to have negative impacts on our families, on our co-workers, and on our social relationships.

Misallocation of resources

Resources are necessary to produce goods and services to satisfy society's wants. These resources are limited and should be used wisely. The more productive use we put them to, the better off we will be. False hope causes people to use resources in pursuits that have no reasonable chance of success, and robs society of a higher standard of living.

Bad choices

False hopes can lead to bad choices. The following illustrative example will make the point. At age 16, Peter entertained the hope of becoming a famous baseball star, earning millions of dollars by the age of 25 years. He devoted much of his time to sports, mainly baseball, and paid little attention to the academics. After high school, Peter was offered an opportunity to turn professional. Without much thought, he accepted, giving up any chance of a college education. In less than a year as a professional baseball player, Peter suffered an injury that prevented him from pursuing a career in baseball. Our last account of Peter was that he was a ticket collector at the Fairmount Amusement Park. Because of the false hope of earning millions of dollars as a baseball player, Peter chose to give up on his academics.

Loss of self-confidence

False hope causes people to pursue objectives that are not realistically achievable. The constant failure to hit unrealizable targets leads to self-doubt and loss of self-confidence which leads to feelings of sadness, stress, depression, anxiety, anger, shame, and guilt.

Bible Verses on False Hope

The Bible is not silent when it comes to false hope; far from it. Several passages of scripture relate to false hope. In this section, we present just a few verses. Some of them are warnings which we would do well to heed.

Instruct those who are rich in this present world not to be conceited or to fix their hope on the uncertainty of riches, but on God, who richly supplies us with all things to enjoy. **(1 Timothy 6:17)**

A horse is a false hope for victory; Nor does it deliver anyone by its great strength. **(Psalm 33:17)**

Let no one deceive you with empty words, for because of these things the wrath of God comes upon the sons of disobedience. **(Ephesians 5:6)**

Hope deferred makes the heart sick, but a desire fulfilled is a tree of life. **(Proverbs 13:12)**

See to it that no one takes you captive by philosophy and empty deceit, according to human tradition, according to the elemental spirits of the world, and not according to Christ. **(Colossians 2:8)**

Overcoming False Hope

As we have seen, false hope has some undesirable consequences. Therefore, overcoming false hope can improve people's lives. There is a three-step process that I have labeled the ACD (Acceptance, Commitment, Decision) technique that will help you overcome false hope.

The ACD Technique

The ACD technique is summarized below.

A = Acceptance

First, recognize and accept reality for what it is. The probability of winning that particular lottery is 1/500,000. Therefore, accept the fact that you are being unreasonable to entertain high hopes of walking away with $5,000,000.

C = Commitment

Second, make a full and sincere commitment to an optimistic but realistic approach that will propel you forward, while resisting the urge to spend resources in futile repetition of the past.

Pathways to a Brighter Future

D = Decision

Third, make a firm decision to act on your commitment, and let nothing deter you from the path you have chosen.

Prayer

We come to You, dear Father, to thank You for Your many blessings. We understand that false hope can be problematic, and in Your word, you have warned us of the dangers of false hope. Help us, dear God, not to fall prey to false hope, but to place our hope in You.

Amen

CHAPTER 5: SALVATION AND HOPE

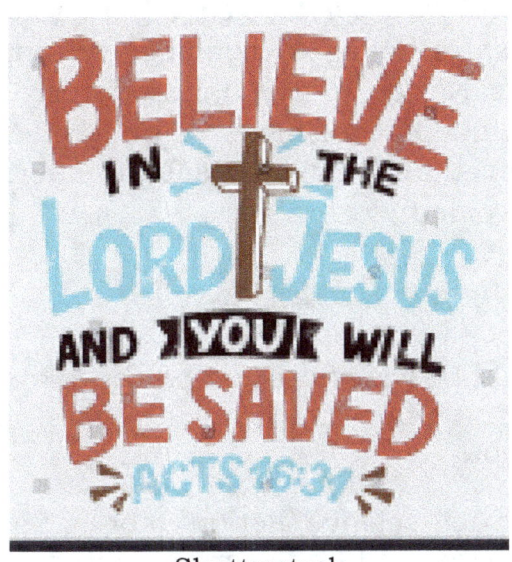

Shutterstock

We obtain salvation by believing in Jesus Christ.

Blessed be the God and Father of our Lord Jesus Christ! According to his great mercy, he has caused us to be born again to a living hope through the resurrection of Jesus Christ from the dead (1 Peter 1:3).

Definition of Salvation

Salvation may mean different things to different people, but for our purpose, we define salvation as the state of being rescued, delivered, or preserved, or freed from ruin, loss, harm, or danger, but especially from sin and its consequences. In this context, what is being delivered or saved is the human soul. A theological discussion of the meaning of the soul need not detain us here. Suffice it to say that the soul is the spiritual part of a human being that gives life to the body.

A useful way to get a clearer understanding of the concept of salvation is to consider its opposite. The opposite of salvation is damnation, which is a state of being condemned to torment in an unpleasant place. Whereas salvation should be sought after, damnation should be avoided.

Sayings about Salvation

It would be wise to reflect on the following sayings about salvation since they give us different perspectives on the subject.

Individual science fiction stories may seem as trivial as ever to the blinder critics and philosophers of today - but the core of science fiction, its essence has become crucial to our salvation if we are to be saved at all. **Isaac Asimov**

It is more noble to give yourself completely to one individual than to labor diligently for the salvation of the masses. **Dag Hammarskjold**

No man is excluded from calling upon God, the gate of salvation is set open unto all men: neither is there any other thing which keepeth us back from entering in, save only our own unbelief. **John Calvin**

The Bible is one of the greatest blessings bestowed by God on the children of men. It has God for its author; salvation for its end, and truth without any mixture for its matter. It is all pure. **John Locke**

There is never time in the future in which we will work out our salvation. The challenge is in the moment; the time is always now. **James Baldwin**

To know yourself as the Being underneath the thinker, the stillness underneath the mental noise, the love and joy underneath the pain, is freedom, salvation, enlightenment. **Eckhart Tolle**

Courage is a kind of salvation. **Plato**

The greatest enemy to human souls is the self-righteous spirit which makes men look to themselves for salvation. **Charles Spurgeon**

Three things are necessary for the salvation of man: to know what he ought to believe; to know what he ought to desire; and to know what he ought to do. **Thomas Aquinas**

I was born into the world as the king of truth for the salvation of the world. **Buddha**

Source: https://www.brainyquote.com/quotes/thomas_aquinas_186902

The Bible on Salvation

In the sayings above, John Locke noted that God is the author of the Bible and that its ultimate goal is salvation. It behooves us then to pay some attention to what the Bible says about salvation.

For by grace you have been saved through faith. And this is not your own doing; it is the gift of God, not a result of works, so that no one may boast. **(Ephesians 2:8-9)**

Because, if you confess with your mouth that Jesus is Lord and believe in your heart that God raised him from the dead, you will be saved. **(Romans 10:9)**

He saved us, not because of works done by us in righteousness, but according to his own mercy, by the washing of regeneration and renewal of the Holy Spirit. **(Titus 3:5)**

And there is salvation in no one else, for there is no other name under heaven given among men by which we must be saved. **(Acts 4:12)**

Then he brought them out and said, "Sirs, what must I do to be saved?" And they said, "Believe in the Lord Jesus, and you will be saved, you and your household." And they spoke the word of the Lord to him and to all who were in his house. And he took them the same hour of the night and washed their wounds; and he was baptized at once, he and all his family. **(Acts 16:30-33)**

The salvation of the righteous is from the Lord; he is their stronghold in the time of trouble. **(Psalm 37:39)**

For God so loved the world, that he gave his only Son, that whoever believes in him should not perish but have eternal life. For God did not send his Son into the world to condemn the world, but in order that the world might be saved through him. Whoever believes in him is not condemned, but whoever does not believe is condemned already, because he has not believed in the name of the only Son of God. **(John 3:16-18)**

Salvation belongs to the Lord; your blessing be on your people! **(Psalm 3:8)**

Therefore let it be known to you that this salvation of God has been sent to the Gentiles; they will listen. **(Acts 28:28)**

Whoever believes and is baptized will be saved, but whoever does not believe will be condemned. **(Mark 16:16)**

Because, if you confess with your mouth that Jesus is Lord and believe in your heart that God raised him from the dead, you will be saved. For with the heart one believes and is justified, and with the mouth one confesses and is saved. **(Romans 10:9-10)**

But I with the voice of thanksgiving will sacrifice to you; what I have vowed I will pay. Salvation belongs to the Lord! **(Jonah 2:9)**

Who Needs Salvation?

Let us see if we can offer a logical response to this very important question. The Bible says we all were born in sin and shaped in iniquity (Psalm 51:5) which means we have a sinful nature. Furthermore, the Apostle Paul says in Romans 3:23 that: "all have sinned and fall short of the glory of God." This position is supported in 1 John 1:8 which reads: "If we claim to be without sin, we deceive ourselves and the truth is not in us." Since we have all sinned, then we have all disobeyed God's laws. When we disobey God's commandments, we expose ourselves to the consequences of sin and therefore need to be rescued, or delivered. This applies to everyone…the entire human race. All the nations of the earth need salvation.

The Cost of Salvation

Many would be willing to pay huge sums of money to free themselves of the consequences of sin and to attain salvation. In a very real sense, the cost of salvation is whatever you must give up to avoid damnation. Sin may have certain temporary pleasures, but you must give them up in order to be saved. On a different level, however, salvation is freely given. The only thing one has to do is to accept it. As children, we used to sing the following chorus:

"If salvation was a thing that money could buy,

Praise ye the Lord,

The rich would live and the poor would die,

Praise ye the Lord."

In his epistle to the Ephesians, Paul described salvation as a *gift* of God by grace through faith, and not something that is earned.

"For by grace you have been saved through faith. And this is not your own doing; it is the gift of God, not a result of works, so that no one may boast." (Ephesians 2:8-9).

Let us willingly accept this offer of salvation that is so freely offered.

Free but not Cheap

In most modern nations, education up to the secondary level is provided by the government free of charge to the direct recipients—students. Similarly, certain services are provided free of charge to selected members of the community, for example, the elderly and children. Such services are free in the sense that they are not paid for directly by the recipients, but they are far from cheap. Expenditures on these items account for a substantial portion of the government's budget. They are free but not cheap.

One of the most popular verses in the Bible tells us:

"For God so loved the world that he gave his one and only Son, that whoever believes in him shall not perish but have eternal life." (John 3:16)

Our salvation was made possible by the cruel death of Jesus, the Son of God, on Calvary's cross. There is nothing cheap about the life of the Son of God, but it was freely given to rescue humankind from the burden of sin and damnation. Salvation is free but not cheap.

Steps to Salvation

There are many people who subscribe to the idea of steps to salvation. The idea of following certain procedures to obtain salvation is appealing to them. Let us examine a few of these *steps* to salvation, beginning with hearing.

Hearing

It is often stated that hearing the good news of salvation is a vital first step in the process. Romans 10:14-15 emphasizes the importance of hearing:

Pathways to a Brighter Future

"How then shall they call on him in whom they have not believed? and how shall they believe in him whom they have not heard? and how shall they hear without a preacher? and how shall they preach, except they be sent?"

But hearing will be of little or no avail unless we act appropriately upon what we hear. It is also of crucial importance that what we hear is the truth. So hearing is not enough.

Repentance

Repentance is feeling sorry for wrongdoing. If we feel remorse for offences that we have committed, the likelihood that we will re-offend is reduced.

"No, I tell you; but unless you repent, you will all likewise perish." (Luke 13:3)

Being penitent is a necessary condition, but it is not sufficient.

Confession

Confession is an admission of having done wrong. If you steal money and are caught, and you confess to having committed the offence, the confession does not set you free from the penalty of the law.

"If we confess our sins, he is faithful and just to forgive us our sins and to cleanse us from all unrighteousness." (1 John 1:9)

Here also, confession is not enough to secure our salvation.

Baptism

Baptism is the Christian ritual of immersing someone in water symbolizing a public demonstration that the person has renounced a sinful way of life and decided to walk in newness of life with Christ. Read what the Bible says in Mark 16:16.

"Whoever believes and is baptized will be saved, but whoever does not believe will be condemned."

Like hearing, repentance, and confession, baptism is necessary but by itself, it is not sufficient. More will be said about baptism in Chapter 12.

What Must I Do to Be Saved?

This was the very question that the Philippian jailer asked Paul and Silas when they were cast into prison. At Philippi, Paul cast a spirit of divination from a young unmarried woman. Consequently, he and his companion Silas were brought before the magistrates who ordered that they be beaten and thrown into prison. At midnight, Paul and Silas were praying and singing praises to God, and there was a great earthquake and everyone's bands were loosed. When the jailer awoke and saw that the doors of the prison were opened, he drew his sword to kill himself, believing that the prisoners had escaped. But Paul shouted, "Do thyself no harm: for we are all here."

Then he brought them out and said, "Sirs, what must I do to be saved?" And they said, "Believe in the Lord Jesus, and you will be saved, you and your household." (Acts 16:30, 31).

See also John 8:24 which says:

"I said therefore unto you, that ye shall die in your sins: for if ye believe not that I am he, ye shall die in your sins."

It seems simple enough. Belief in Jesus is **the** *necessary* **and** *sufficient* condition for salvation. Because we are saved by believing in the name of Jesus, we repent, we confess, and we get baptized.

Hope of Salvation

The following hymn is an excellent example of how the hope of salvation can buoy the human spirit up. It is called, "I Saw One Weary."

I Saw One Weary

1
I saw one weary, sad, and torn,
With eager steps press on the way,
Who long the hallowed cross had born,
Still looking for the promised day;
While many a line of grief and care,
Upon his brow was furrowed there;
I asked what buoyed his spirits up,
"O this" said he - "the blessed hope."

2
And one I saw, with sword and shield,
Who boldly braved the world's cold frown,
And fought, unyielding, on the field,
To win an everlasting crown.
Though worn with toil, oppressed by foes,
No murmur from his heart arose;
I asked what buoyed his spirits up,

HOPE

"O this!" said he - "the blessed hope."

3
And there was one who left behind
The cherished friends of early years,
And honor, pleasure, wealth resigned,
To tread the path bedewed with tears.
Through trials deep and conflict sore,
Yet still a smile of joy he wore;
I asked what buoyed his spirits up,
"O this!" said he - "the blessed hope."
4
While pilgrims here we journey on
In this dark vale of sin and gloom,
Through tribulation, hate, and scorn,
Or through the portals of the tomb,
Till our returning King shall come
To take His exile captives home,
O! what can bouy the spirits up?
'Tis this alone - the blessed hope. **(Annie R. Smith)**

The above hymn is about the blessed hope. But what exactly is the blessed hope? And what does it have to do with salvation? The blessed hope is the anticipated joyous return of Jesus as revealed in Titus 2:12, 13:

"Teaching us that, denying ungodliness and worldly lusts, we should live soberly, righteously, and godly, in this present world; Looking for that blessed hope, and the glorious appearing of the great God and our Saviour Jesus Christ."

In John 14:3, Jesus promised that He would return:

Pathways to a Brighter Future

"And if I go and prepare a place for you, I will come back and take you to be with me that you also may be where I am."

In Acts 1:11, at Jesus' ascension, the angels declared that He would return.

"Men of Galilee," they said, "why do you stand here looking into the sky? This same Jesus, who has been taken from you into heaven, will come back in the same way you have seen him go into heaven."

So we live with this hope that one day, Jesus will return to this earth to take us home to be with Him forevermore. There will be no more sorrow, no more pain, no more sickness, no more unbearable separations, no more death. We will be saved forevermore.

*We have this hope that burns within our heart,
Hope in the coming of the Lord.
We have this faith that Christ alone imparts,
Faith in the promise of His Word.
We believe the time is here,
When the nations far and near
Shall awake, and shout and sing
Hallelujah! Christ is King!
We have this hope that burns within our heart,
Hope in the coming of the Lord.* **(Wayne H. Hooper)**

If indeed we have this blessed hope burning in our hearts, our lives should exemplify the life of Christ. **(1 John3:3)**.

"All who have this hope in him purify themselves, just as he is pure."

Prayer

Father in heaven, we have sinned. We have done things that we ought not to have done, and we have neglected to do things that we should have done. Sin has separated us from you, and we are sorry. Father, forgive us of our transgressions and save us in your kingdom.

Amen

Pathways to a Brighter Future

CHAPTER 6: REDEMPTION

Pixabay

It is Jesus who redeemed our souls from sin.

I have blotted out, as a thick cloud, thy transgressions, and, as a cloud, thy sins: return unto me; for I have redeemed thee (Isaiah 44:22).

In the previous chapter, we devoted some time to the study of Salvation. We noted that since we have all sinned and fallen short of the glory of God, then all of us need salvation. We emphasized the point that salvation was free and can be obtained only by believing in Jesus Christ. In the present chapter, we turn our attention to the closely related but different concept of redemption. Let us begin by defining redemption.

Definition of Redemption

Redemption is the act of purchasing back, or reclaiming, something or someone. For example, if, at a garage sale, someone mistakenly sold you a picture that was not supposed to be sold for $5.00, and then discovers the error, he or she may offer $15 as a redemption. Within the realm of Christianity, it is the soul that is bought back or redeemed from sin. Clearly, a close relationship exists between salvation and redemption. In the following section, we look at that relationship. By so doing, we hope to enhance our understanding of each concept.

The Relationship between Salvation and Redemption

Often, many Christians use salvation and redemption as synonymous terms. For example, one may say: "Salvation is offered freely by the blood of the Lamb." Another, voicing a similar sentiment, may proclaim: "Redemption is obtained through the precious blood of Jesus." Although both statements are true in general, there is a technical difference between the two concepts.

Salvation generally refers to the act of being rescued or delivered from some form of harm, danger, or negative consequences. In religious contexts, it often refers to the process by which a person is saved or delivered from sin, spiritual death, or eternal separation from God. Salvation is seen as a gift or grace offered by God to humanity.

As we have seen in the previous chapter, salvation is freely offered by Jesus. Although it is free, it is not cheap. Christ died on the cross so that we can obtain salvation from the clutches of sin. Salvation thus obtained enables Christians to live a life that is in accordance with God's will.

Redemption, on the other hand, as specified above, refers specifically to the action of buying back or repurchasing or reclaiming something that was lost. Technically, it involves paying a price to reclaim or redeem someone or something. In Christianity, it is associated with reclaiming someone from sin so that he or she can return to the fold of God.

We can firmly state then the salvation is closely related to redemption. The belief is that Jesus' sacrificial death on Calvary's cross served as the ultimate act of redemption, paying the price for humanity's sins and providing a way for people to be reconciled with God.

To summarize, it may be observed that while salvation and redemption are both about deliverance and restoration, salvation generally refers to the broader concept of being saved or rescued from sin and its negative consequences, whereas redemption focuses specifically on the act of being bought back or reclaimed, often through the payment of a price. In religious contexts, both terms are often used in conjunction with the idea of being saved from sin and its consequences.

The Bible on Redemption

We believe that the Bible is the immutable word of God, therefore we place great faith in its teachings. In this section, we list some Bible verses that relate to redemption.

In him we have redemption through his blood, the forgiveness of our respasses, according to the riches of his grace, **(Ephesians 1:7)**

In whom we have redemption, the forgiveness of sins. **(Colossians 1:14)**

who gave himself for us to redeem us from all lawlessness and to purify for himself a people for his own possession who are zealous for good works. **(Titus 2:14)**

He sent redemption to his people; he has commanded his covenant forever.
Holy and awesome is his name! **(Psalm 111:9)**

knowing that you were ransomed from the futile ways inherited from your forefathers, not with perishable things such as silver or gold, but with the precious blood of Christ, like that of a lamb without blemish or spot. **(1 Peter 1:18-19)**

O Israel, hope in the LORD! For with the LORD there is steadfast love, and with him is plentiful redemption. **(Psalm 130:7)**

And because of him you are in Christ Jesus, who became to us wisdom from God, righteousness and sanctification and redemption, **(1 Corinthians 1:30)**

for you were bought with a price. So glorify God in your body. **(1 Corinthians 6:20)**

Pathways to a Brighter Future

and are justified by his grace as a gift, through the redemption that is in Christ Jesus, whom God put forward as a propitiation by his blood, to be received by faith. This was to show God's righteousness, because in his divine forbearance he had passed over former sins. It was to show his righteousness at the present time, so that he might be just and the justifier of the one who has faith in Jesus. **(Romans 3:24-26)**

he entered once for all into the holy places, not by means of the blood of goats and calves but by means of his own blood, thus securing an eternal redemption. **(Hebrews 9:12)**

I have blotted out your transgressions like a cloud and your sins like mist; return to me, for I have redeemed you. **(Isaiah 44:22)**

Let the redeemed of the LORD say so, whom he has redeemed from trouble **(Psalm 107:2)**

Christ redeemed us from the curse of the law by becoming a curse for us—for it is written, "Cursed is everyone who is hanged on a tree"— **(Galatians 3:13)**

Therefore he is the mediator of a new covenant, so that those who are called may receive the promised eternal inheritance, since a death has occurred that redeems them from the transgressions committed under the first covenant. **(Hebrews 9:15)**

To redeem those who were under the law, so that we might receive adoption as sons. **(Galatians 4:5)**

You were bought with a price; do not become bondservants of men. **(1 Corinthians 7:23)**

And they sang a new song, saying, "Worthy are you to take the scroll and to open its seals, for you were *slain, and by your blood you ransomed people for God from every tribe and language and people and nation,* **(Revelation 5:9)**

even as the Son of Man came not to be served but to serve, and to give his life as a ransom for many." **(Matthew 20:28)**

who gave himself as a ransom for all, which is the testimony given at the proper time. **(1 Timothy 2:6)**

The central message of Scripture is that Jesus Christ redeemed us through His precious blood.

Sayings about Redemption

We can be enlightened by what others have to say about redemption even though we may not agree with the sentiments expressed. Here are some sayings:

"Mere improvement is not redemption, though redemption always improves people." **C. S. Lewis**

"I think redemption is about righting a wrong, and in that pursuit it's about trying. You can stumble, you can make mistakes, but it's about trying to do the right thing." **Michael B. Jordan**

"No human being is so bad as to be beyond redemption." **Mahatma Gandhi**

"I tell you to keep going, not because it's easy. Not because it doesn't hurt. I tell you to keep going because there's no other way. To stop is to die. Life is in motion. In growth. In change. Life is in seeking and in finding. Life is in redemption. Each moment is a new birth. A new chance to come back, to get it right. A new chance to make it better." **Yasmin Mogahed**

Pathways to a Brighter Future

"Everything which is done in the present, affects the future by consequence, and the past by redemption." **Paulo Coelho**

"Love has within it a redemptive power. And there is a power there that eventually transforms individuals. Just keep being friendly to that person. Just keep loving them, and they can't stand it too long. Oh, they react in many ways in the beginning. They react with guilt feelings, and sometimes they'll hate you a little more at that transition period, but just keep loving them. And by the power of your love they will break down under the load. That's love, you see. It is redemptive." **Martin Luther King, Jr.**

"Redemption comes to those who wait, forgiveness is the key." **Tom Petty**

"The cost of redemption cannot be overstated. The wonders of grace cannot be overemphasized. Christ took the hell He didn't deserve so we could have the heaven we don't deserve." **Randy Alcorn**

"God is the ultimate musician. His music transforms your life. The notes of redemption rearrange your heart and restore your life. His songs of forgiveness, grace, reconciliation, truth, hope, sovereignty, and love give you back your humanity and restore your identity." **Paul David Tripp**

"Seeking to forget makes exile all the longer; the secret of redemption lies in remembrance." **Richard von Weizsaecker**

"Action is redemption." **Emily Dickinson**

"Perseverance, determination, commitment, and courage-those things are real. The desire for redemption drives you." **Michael Phelps**

"Redemption just means you just make a change in your life and you try to do right, versus what you were doing, which was wrong." **Ice T**

"Sleep is the interest we have to pay on the capital which is called in at death; and the higher the rate of interest and the more regularly it is paid, the further the date of redemption is postponed."**Arthur Schopenhauer**

"Failure is an option. It's what you do with the failure that makes you who you are. Our failures mold us. I have failed at several things in my life. What sets some of us apart, is that when we fail, we can't sleep at night. It haunts us until we have our time at redemption." **David Goggins**

"The heart of the gospel is redemption, and the essence of redemption is the substitutionary sacrifice of Christ." **Charles Spurgeon**

"Look to the Heavens, you can look to the skies. You can find redemption staring back into your eyes." **Josh Turner**

"Of course, we do the righteous deed because of our redemption, not for our redemption." **Dallas Willard**

"You cannot amputate your history from your destiny, because that is redemption." **Beth Moore**

"If Jesus Christ was who He claimed to be, and He did die on a cross at a point of time in history, then, for all history past and all history future it is relevant because that is the very focal point for forgiveness and redemption." **Josh McDowell**

"Jesus Christ is both the only price and sacrifice by which eternal redemption is obtained for believers." **Jonathan Edwards**

"Hell is yourself and the only redemption is when a person puts himself aside to feel deeply for another person." **Tennessee Williams**

Source: https://www.azquotes.com/quotes/topics/redemption.html

The Story of Redemption

The story of redemption is fascinating. God is omniscient, knowing everything from beginning to end. He knew that Lucifer would have rebelled against His government and be thrown out of heaven. He knew that the Devil would succeed in getting Adam and Eve to disobey Him and eat the forbidden fruit. The Fall of mankind in the Garden of Eden was no surprise to our all-knowing God. A rescue plan was already in place. That plan was the plan of redemption.

Here, in essence, is the story of redemption. Adam and Eve sinned by disobeying God (Genesis 3:1-6). As a result, humankind is born in sin and shaped in iniquity (Psalm 51:5). And since the wages of sin is death (Romans 6:23), the soul that sins must surely die (Ezekiel 18:20). How can our relationship with the Father be restored? How can we be redeemed? God sent His only begotten son, Jesus, born of a virgin, Mary, to die in our stead, so that we may live and not die. God paid the price. The following song tells the story.

JUST SUPPOSE

Just suppose God searched through Heaven,
And couldn't find one willing to be,
The supreme sacrifice that was needed,
That would buy eternal life for you and me

HOPE

Had it not been for a place called Mount Calvary,
Had it not been for the old rugged cross,
Had it not been for a man called Jesus,
Then forever my soul would be lost

Well I'm so glad He was willing to drink His bitter cup,
Although He prayed "Father let it pass from me",
And I'm so glad He never called Heaven's angels,
From these hands, Pulled the nails that torment me
Rusty Goodman

Yes, He paid the supreme price that was needed as a ransom for you and me.

Let us not forget that:

Jesus paid it all
All to him I owe
Sin had left a crimson stain
He washed it white as snow

And when before the throne
I stand in him complete
Jesus died my soul to save
My lips shall still repeat
Alex Nifong

    The crucial point of the redemption story is Jesus' sacrificial death on Calvary's cross. It is recorded vividly in the gospel of John:

    Then the soldiers, when they had crucified Jesus, took his garments, and made four parts, to every soldier a part; and also his coat: now the coat was without seam, woven from the top throughout. They said therefore among themselves, Let us not rend it, but cast lots for it, whose it shall be: that the scripture might be fulfilled, which saith, They parted my raiment among them, and for my vesture they did cast lots. These things therefore the soldiers did. Now there stood by the cross of Jesus his mother, and his mother's sister, Mary the wife of Cleophas, and Mary Magdalene. When Jesus therefore saw his mother, and the disciple standing by, whom he loved, he saith unto his mother, Woman, behold thy son! Then saith he to the disciple, Behold thy mother! And from that hour that disciple took her unto his own home.

After this, Jesus knowing that all things were now accomplished, that the scripture might be fulfilled, saith, I thirst.

Now there was set a vessel full of vinegar: and they filled a sponge with vinegar, and put it upon hyssop, and put it to his mouth.

When Jesus therefore had received the vinegar, he said, It is finished: and he bowed his head, and gave up the ghost. **(John 19:23-30)**

When Jesus said, "It is finished", He gave the assurance that His mission was accomplished. Human's redemption was paid. He has redeemed us. One Bible verse adequately sums up the Story of Redemption:

"For God so loved the world that he gave his one and only Son, that whoever believes in him shall not perish but have eternal life." (John 3:16)

Hope and Redemption

Hope and redemption are powerful concepts that resonate deeply within the human spirit. In the face of adversity and despair, hope serves as a guiding light, a beacon that inspires individuals to keep moving forward with optimism. It is the belief that there is a possibility for a brighter future, even when circumstances seem bleak. Hope breathes life into dreams, encouraging people to strive for something better, to reach beyond their limitations, and to find the strength to overcome obstacles. It is a force that can mend broken hearts, heal wounded souls, and provide the courage needed to embark on a journey of redemption.

Redemption, on the other hand, is deliverance from the bondage of sin through the blood of Christ. With redemption, we are free to pursue a path that leads to righteousness and the accomplishment of the things we hope for—peace, honesty, happiness, love, excellent relationships, harmony, and eventually eternal life with Jesus, our Redeemer.

Together, hope and redemption form a profound and transformative narrative. They remind us that even in the darkest moments, there is a glimmer of light. They urge us to confront our flaws and acknowledge our imperfections, understanding that everyone is capable of change and deserving of a second chance. Hope fuels the pursuit of redemption, as the belief in a better tomorrow encourages individuals to confront their past and work towards a more positive future. Ultimately, hope and redemption are a testament to the strength of the human spirit and the capacity for growth and renewal that resides within each of us, through Jesus Christ our redeemer.

Redeemed

Redeemed, how I love to proclaim it!
Redeemed by the blood of the Lamb;
Redeemed through His infinite mercy,
His child, and forever, I am.

Refrain:
Redeemed, redeemed,
Redeemed by the blood of the Lamb;
Redeemed, how I love to proclaim it!
His child, and forever, I am.

I think of my blessed Redeemer,
I think of Him all the day long;
I sing, for I cannot be silent;
His love is the theme of my song.

I know I shall see in His beauty
The King in whose law I delight,
Who lovingly guardeth my footsteps,
And giveth me songs in the night.
Fanny Crosby

The above hymn nicely summarizes the gratitude and the joy of the redeemed.

When the angels sing "Holy, Holy", the redeemed of earth will join in the heavenly chorus, but the angels will not be able to join in the singing of Redemption Story because they have never been redeemed. This is how Johnson Oatman expresses it in the following Redemption Song:

HOLY, HOLY, IS WHAT THE ANGELS SING

1. There is singing up in heaven
such as we have never known,
Where the angels sing the praises
of the Lamb upon the throne;
Their sweet harps are ever tuneful
and their voices are always clear,
O that we might be more like them
while we serve the Master here!

HOPE

Refrain
Holy, holy, is what the angels sing,
And I expect to help them make
the courts of heaven ring;
But when I sing redemption's story,
they will fold their wings,
For angels never felt the joys
that our salvation brings.

2. But I hear another anthem,
blending voices clear and strong,
"Unto Him who hath redeemed us
and hath bought us," is the song;
We have come thro' tribulations
to this land so fair and bright,
In the fountain freely flowing
He hath made our garments white.

3. Then the angels stand and listen,
for they cannot join that song,
Like the sound of many waters,
by that happy, blood-washed throng;
For they sing about great trials,
battles fought and vict'ries won,
And they praised the great Redeemer,
who hath said to them, "Well done."

4. So, although I'm not an angel,
yet I know that over there
I will join a blessed chorus
that the angels cannot share;
I will sing about my Savior,
who upon dark Calvary
Freely pardoned my transgressions,
died to set the sinner free.
Johnson Oatman

Prayer

Oh, how wonderful it is to know that we have been redeemed (bought back)! Father, we thank You for sending Your Son, Jesus to pay the price to ransom us. We pray that, by Your grace, we will show appreciation by serving only You.

Amen

CHAPTER 7: FAITH AND HOPE

We cannot please God without faith.

Through whom also we have obtained our introduction by faith into this grace in which we stand; and we exult in hope of the glory of God (Romans 5:2)

The private secondary school that I attended, and from which I graduated was called Faith and Hope High School. I also knew two sisters, one named Faith and the other named Hope. Perhaps that is one reason why, in my mind, there is a close association between faith and hope. Up to this point, we have examined certain dimensions of hope. In this chapter, we will pay some attention to faith and examine its relationship to hope.

Faith Defined

Faith can be defined as trust or belief in someone or something. For example, you can have faith that your poetry submission will be accepted by the committee. In order to glean a clearer understanding of the meaning of faith, let us look at its antonym—doubt. Doubt is a lack of conviction or faith. If you doubt that she will pass the examination, then you lack faith or belief in her ability to be successful in the examination.

Degrees of Faith

A thorough analysis of the different degrees of faith need not detain us here. Suffice it to say that all faith is not equal. The Bible mentions different degrees of faith. For example, Paul made this suggestion in the following passage of Scripture:

For by the grace given me I say to every one of you: Do not think of yourself more highly than you ought, but rather think of yourself with sober judgment, in accordance with the faith God has distributed to each of you **(Romans 12:3)**

Paul also, in the same Book, when talking about the faith of Abraham, referred to weak faith and strong faith. Here is the passage:

And being not weak in faith, he considered not his own body now dead, when he was about an hundred years old, neither yet the deadness of Sarah's womb: He staggered not at the promise of God through unbelief; but was strong in faith, giving glory to God; **(Romans 4:19-20)**

Finally, we would like to mention another degree of faith, and that is dead faith. We read about dead faith in the Book of James:

In the same way, faith by itself, if it is not accompanied by action, is dead **(James 2:17).**

As the body without the spirit is dead, so faith without deeds is dead **(James 2:26).**

Here, James is defining dead faith as faith that is not manifested by work.

Sayings about Faith

Sayings about faith are numerous. In this section, we list some quotes about faith that may inspire you and help you to see faith from different perspectives. My hope is that after reading these quotes, you will have a deeper understanding of faith.

1. "Faith is not the belief that God will do what you want. It is the belief that God will do what is right." **- Max Lucado**

2. "Have faith in God; God has faith in you." **- Edwin Louis Cole**

3. "Faith is to believe what you do not see; the reward of this faith is to see what you believe." **- Saint Augustine**

4. "Love is an act of faith." **- Erich Fromm**

5. "Faith and prayer are the vitamins of the soul; man cannot live in health without them." **- Mahalia Jackson**

6. "The problem with the world is that the intelligent people are full of doubts, while the stupid ones are full of confidence." - **Charles Bukowski**

7. "To have faith is to trust yourself to the water. When you swim you don't grab hold of the water, because if you do you will sink and drown. Instead you relax, and float." - **Alan Watts**

8. "Faith is the bird that feels the light when the dawn is still dark." -**Rabindranath Tagore**

9. "Faith is not believing that God can. It is knowing that God will." - **Ben Stein**

10. "When you get to the end of all the light you know and it's time to step into the darkness of the unknown, faith is knowing that one of two things shall happen: either you will be given something solid to stand on, or you will be taught how to fly." - **Edward Teller**

11. "Faith sees the invisible, believes the unbelievable, and receives the impossible." - **Corrie ten Boom**

12. "To one who has faith, no explanation is necessary. To one without faith, no explanation is possible." - **Thomas Aquinas**

13. "Faith is a passionate intuition." - **William Wordsworth**

14. "A little faith will bring your soul to heaven; a great faith will bring heaven to your soul." - **Charles H. Spurgeon**

15. "Be faithful in small things because it is in them that your strength lies." - **Mother Teresa**

16. "Faith goes up the stairs that love has built and looks out the windows which hope has opened." - **Charles H. Spurgeon**

17. "Faith is the strength by which a shattered world shall emerge into the light." - **Helen Keller**

18. "Doubt is a pain too lonely to know that faith is his twin brother." -**Khalil Gibran**

19. "In faith there is enough light for those who want to believe and enough shadows to blind those who don't." - **Blaise Pascal**

Source: https://quotefancy.com/faith-quotes

The Bible on Faith

Not surprisingly, the Bible is replete with verses about faith. In the Christian realm, faith in God is of supreme importance. The Old and New Testaments are teeming with instances of faith. One may go as far as to say that faith is the basis of many, if not all, religions. It would be impractical to list all the Bible verses dealing with faith. What follows is a sample of what the Bible has to say about faith. Let us begin with what we will refer to as Faith's Hall of Fame.

Faith's Hall of Fame

Faith's Hall of Fame is a list of Old Testament characters who committed incredible acts of faith and should be honored and remembered as stalwarts in the faith arena. The list is contained in Hebrews 11 as follows:

Pathways to a Brighter Future

Abel: By faith Abel brought God a better offering than Cain did. By faith he was commended as righteous, when God spoke well of his offerings. And by faith Abel still speaks, even though he is dead.

Enoch: By faith Enoch was taken from this life, so that he did not experience death: "He could not be found, because God had taken him away." For before he was taken, he was commended as one who pleased God. And without faith it is impossible to please God, because anyone who comes to him must believe that he exists and that he rewards those who earnestly seek him.

Noah: By faith Noah, when warned about things not yet seen, in holy fear built an ark to save his family. By his faith he condemned the world and became heir of the righteousness that is in keeping with faith.

Abraham: By faith Abraham, when called to go to a place he would later receive as his inheritance, obeyed and went, even though he did not know where he was going. By faith he made his home in the promised land like a stranger in a foreign country; he lived in tents, as did Isaac and Jacob, who were heirs with him of the same promise. For he was looking forward to the city with foundations, whose architect and builder is God.

Sarah: And by faith even Sarah, who was past childbearing age, was enabled to

bear children because she considered him faithful who had made the promise. And so from this one man, and he as good as dead, came descendants as numerous as the stars in the sky and as countless as the sand on the seashore.

All these people were still living by faith when they died. They did not receive the things promised; they only saw them and welcomed them from a distance, admitting that they were foreigners and strangers on earth. People who say such things show that they are looking for a country of their own. If they had been thinking of the country they had left, they would have had an opportunity to return. Instead, they were longing for a better country—a heavenly one. Therefore God is not ashamed to be called their God, for he has prepared a city for them.

Abraham (again): By faith Abraham, when God tested him, offered Isaac as a sacrifice. He who had embraced the promises was about to sacrifice his one and only son, even though God had said to him, "It is through Isaac that your offspring will be reckoned." Abraham reasoned that God could even raise the dead, and so in a manner of speaking he did receive Isaac back from death.

Isaac: By faith Isaac blessed Jacob and Esau in regard to their future.

Jacob: By faith Jacob, when he was dying, blessed each of Joseph's sons, and worshiped as he leaned on the top of his staff.

Joseph: By faith Joseph, when his end was near, spoke about the exodus of the Israelites from Egypt and gave instructions concerning the burial of his bones.

Moses' parents: By faith Moses' parents hid him for three months after he was born, because they saw he was no ordinary child, and they were not afraid of the king's edict.

Moses: By faith Moses, when he had grown up, refused to be known as the son of Pharaoh's daughter. He chose to be mistreated along with the people of God rather than to enjoy the fleeting pleasures of sin. He regarded disgrace for the sake of Christ as of greater value than the treasures of Egypt, because he was looking ahead to his reward. By faith he left Egypt, not fearing the king's anger; he persevered because he saw him who is invisible. By faith he kept the Passover and the application of blood, so that the destroyer of the firstborn would not touch the firstborn of Israel.

The children of Israel: By faith the people passed through the Red Sea as on dry land; but when the Egyptians tried to do so, they were drowned. By faith the walls of Jericho fell, after the army had marched around them for seven days.

Rahab: By faith the prostitute Rahab, because she welcomed the spies, was not killed with those who were disobedient.

Gideon, Barak, Samson, Jephthah, David, Samuel, and others: And what more shall I say? I do not have time to tell about Gideon, Barak, Samson and Jephthah, about David and Samuel and the prophets, who through faith conquered kingdoms, administered justice, and gained what was promised; who shut the mouths of lions, quenched the fury of the flames, and escaped the edge of the sword; whose weakness was turned to strength; and who became powerful in battle and routed foreign armies. Women received back their dead, raised to life again. There were others who were tortured, refusing to be released so that they might gain an even better resurrection. Some faced jeers and flogging, and even chains and imprisonment. They were put to death by stoning; they were sawed in two; they were killed by the sword. They went about in sheepskins and goatskins, destitute, persecuted and mistreated—the world was not worthy of them. They wandered in deserts and mountains, living in caves and in holes in the ground.

These were all commended for their faith, yet none of them received what had been promised, since God had planned something better for us so that only together with us would they be made perfect. **(Hebrews 11:4-40)**

Bible Verses about Faith

Here are some Bible verses about faith.

Therefore I tell you, whatever you ask for in prayer, believe that you have received it, and it will be yours. **(Mark 11:24)**

I pray that out of his glorious riches he may strengthen you with power through his Spirit in your inner being, so that Christ may dwell in your hearts through faith. And I pray that you, being rooted and established in love. **(Ephesians 3:16-17)**

Now faith is confidence in what we hope for and assurance about what we do not see. **(Hebrews 11:1)**

For we live by faith, not by sight. **(2 Corinthians 5:7)**

But when you ask, you must believe and not doubt, because the one who doubts is like a wave of the sea, blown and tossed by the wind. **(James 1:6)**

Then Jesus said, "Did I not tell you that if you believe, you will see the glory of God?" **(John 11:40)**

Pathways to a Brighter Future

Because you know that the testing of your faith produces perseverance. **(James 1:3)**

Though you have not seen him, you love him; and even though you do not see him now, you believe in him and are filled with an inexpressible and glorious joy, for you are receiving the end result of your faith, the salvation of your souls. **(1 Peter 1:8-9)**

For everyone born of God overcomes the world. This is the victory that has overcome the world, even our faith. **(1 John 5:4)**

*Accept the one whose faith is weak, without quarreling over disputable matters. **(Romans 14:1)***

But you, man of God, flee from all this, and pursue righteousness, godliness, faith, love, endurance and gentleness. **(1 Timothy 6:1)**

*"Go," said Jesus, "your faith has healed you." Immediately he received his sight and followed Jesus along the road. **(Mark 10:52)***

If I have the gift of prophecy and can fathom all mysteries and all knowledge, and if I have a faith that can move mountains, but do not have love, I am nothing. **(1 Corinthians 13:2)**

Be on your guard; stand firm in the faith; be courageous; be strong. **(1 Corinthians 16:13)**

For it is with your heart that you believe and are justified, and it is with your mouth that you profess your faith and are saved. **(Romans 10:10)**

Is anyone among you sick? Let them call the elders of the church to pray over them and anoint them with oil in the name of the Lord. And the prayer offered in faith will make the sick person well; the Lord will raise them up. If they have sinned, they will be forgiven. **(James 5:14-15)**

For in the gospel the righteousness of God is revealed—a righteousness that is by faith from first to last, just as it is written: "The righteous will live by faith." **(Romans 1:17)**

So in Christ Jesus you are all children of God through faith. **(Galatians 3:26)**

The Importance of Faith in Our Lives

Faith plays an important role in our daily lives. Space does not allow us to enumerate all the benefits that faith bestows upon people, but we will point out some of the advantages of having faith.

Faith gives confidence

If you have a certain task to perform, such as running a race in a given time, or learning a certain skill, having faith in your ability to accomplish the task, will give you the motivation to tackle it with confidence, and this will go a long way towards helping you to be successful.

Faith prompts you to action

Five-year-old Sam ran at full speed and jumped into his father's waiting arms, without any doubt whatever that his father would catch him. Faith obliterates any doubt that might inhibit action. You are probably familiar with the proverb, "Nothing ventured, nothing gained." Faith allows us to venture out in order to gain.

Faith can unite people

People who have common beliefs on certain issues tend to be drawn together, and it is well-known that unity is strength. The adage that birds of a feather flock together applies in this case. Faith gives a sense of community. As people share their beliefs, they tend to grow stronger. It's a case of iron sharpening iron. Not only does your faith grow stronger, but so does the faith of those with whom you share.

Faith helps people overcome difficulties

As we go through life's journey, we face difficulties and challenges of various types. Some of them threaten our ability to move forward. Because of faith, we can dig deep and find the resilience to overcome the stumbling blocks that interfere with our drive to victory.

Faith adds positivity to life

When in doubt, faith steps in and says, "I can do it." This positive attitude that faith brings to our lives can help us in innumerable ways. A positive worldview helps us to deal effectively with the vicissitudes of life, so that the negative impacts are minimized.

Relationship between Faith and Hope

There can be no doubt that hope and faith are closely related. Hope needs faith, and faith needs hope. It seems as if people have hope because they have faith, and they have faith because they have hope. In Chapter 1 of this book, we defined hope as "a state of optimism originating from the expectation that some desired outcome will materialize", and earlier in this chapter, we defined faith as "a strong belief, trust, or confidence in someone or something that is neither verified nor based on proof." The concepts are similar but different. The Apostle Paul puts it this way:

"Faith is the confidence that what we hope for will actually happen; it gives us assurance about things we cannot see." (Hebrews 11:1)

Faithful Christians have complete belief in Jesus Christ, and this faith gives us hope that He will return to this earth because He has promised. Clearly, faith and hope are interrelated. Faith does not exist without hope, and hope does not exist without faith.

The following example will help to illustrate the complementary nature of faith and hope. Imagine the joy that a child feels when his mother informs him that his favorite grandmother is going to visit. Because he has faith in his mother, he believes wholeheartedly that the visit will occur. The optimistic anticipation of the expected visit is hope.

Pathways to a Brighter Future

Inspirational Hymn about Faith

It is hoped that the following hymn about faith will serve as an inspiration.

1. Faith of our fathers, living still
In spite of dungeon, fire and sword,
O how our hearts beat high with joy
Whene'er we hear that glorious word!
Faith of our fathers! holy faith!
We will be true to thee till death!

2. Our fathers, chained in prisons dark,
Were still in heart and conscience free;
And blest would be their children's fate,
If they, like them should die for thee:
Faith of our fathers! holy faith!
We will be true to thee till death!

3. Faith of our fathers, we will strive
To win all nations unto thee;
And through the truth that comes from God
Mankind shall then indeed be free.
Faith of our fathers! holy faith!
We will be true to thee till death!

4. Faith of our fathers, we will love
Both friend and foe in all our strife,
And preach thee, too, as love knows how
By kindly words and virtuous life.
Faith of our fathers! holy faith!
We will be true to thee till death!

Frederick William Faber

Prayer

Father in Heaven, our Saviour, our Redeemer, we surrender ourselves completely to you. Your wish for us is that we prosper and be in good health. It is Your wish that we will be where You are. We realize that our lack of faith is blocking your blessings from reaching us. Increase our faith, Father, so that Your wish for us will be manifested. We pray in the name of Jesus.

Amen

Pathways to a Brighter Future

CHAPTER 8: PRAYER

The image is the familiar hands indicating a symbol of prayer.

Do not be anxious about anything, but in every situation, by prayer and petition, with thanksgiving, present your requests to God. And the peace of God, which transcends all understanding, will guard your hearts and your minds in Christ Jesus. (Philippians 4:6-7)

Prayer is probably the most powerful weapon that Christians have against the enemy, Satan. Prayer increases our faith in God, strengthens our relationship with Him, increases our ability to communicate with Him, calms our fears, and causes us to know Him better. In this chapter, we shall focus on prayer so that we can gain a more comprehensive understanding of this practice. We will examine what some people say about prayer, what the Bible reveals to us about prayer, the model prayer of Jesus, some great pray-ers in the Bible, and a few notable prayers recorded in the Bible. Finally, we will examine the relationship between hope and prayer.

What is Prayer?

Let us begin with a definition of prayer. Notice we mention **a** definition rather than **the** definition of prayer. This suggests that one may use different words to state the same concept. Britannica defines prayer as follows:

***Prayer**, an act of communication by humans with the sacred or holy—God, the gods, the transcendent realm, or supernatural powers. Found in all religions in all times, prayer may be a corporate or personal act utilizing various forms and techniques.*

The Oxford Dictionary defines prayer as:

a solemn request for help or expression of thanks addressed to God or another deity.

I have often heard people say, "I can't pray very well", or "I don't know how to pray", or, "I say my prayers but I don't really think that's the same as praying. It is important to know that prayer does not require sophisticated language and correct grammar and syntax. We can all talk to God, our Father, in whatever manner we can, and He will hear us and listen to us.

Sayings about Prayer

Although our focus is on what the Word of God says about prayer, the sayings of people shed some light on their views on prayers that might give us pause to think about the practice. Here are some sayings about prayer. Some are humorous and lighthearted while others are sobering, thought-provoking, and convey deep spiritual truths.

Don't worry about having the right words; worry more about having the right heart. It's not eloquence he seeks, just honesty. **Max Lucado**

[Prayer] is the link between God's inexhaustible resources and people's needs...God is the source of power, but we are the instrument He uses to link the two together. **Charles Stanley**

The idea seemed to be that if you prayed extremely hard--especially if a lot of people prayed at once--maybe God would change things. The trouble was, what if your enemy was praying, too? Which prayer would God listen to? **Jeanne DuPrau**

The Holy Spirit as the Spirit of Power helpeth our infirmity in prayer. The Holy Spirit as the Spirit of Life ends our deadness in prayer. The Holy Spirit as the Spirit of Wisdom delivers us from ignorance in this holy art of prayer. The Holy Spirit as the Spirit of Fire delivers us from coldness in prayer. The Holy Spirit as the Spirit of Might comes to our aid in our weakness as we pray. **Leonard Ravenhill**

But who prays for Satan? Who, in eighteen centuries, has had the common humanity to pray for the one sinner that needed it most? **Mark Twain**

To pray is to accept that we are, and always will be, wholly dependent on God for everything. **Timothy Keller**

HOPE

For prayer is nothing else than being on terms of friendship with God. **Teresa of Avila**

Prayer is as natural an expression of faith as breathing is of life. **Jonathan Edwards**

To pray without expectation is to misunderstand the whole concept of prayer and relationship with God. **Aiden Wilson Tozer**

Prayer may not change things for you, but it for sure changes you for things. **Sam Shoemaker**

Persistent calling upon the name of the Lord breaks through every stronghold of the devil, for nothing is impossible with God. For Christians in these troubled times there is simply no other way. **Jim Cymbala**

Intercession is the truly universal work for the Christian. No place is closed to intercessory prayer: no continent, no nation, no city, no organization, no office. No power on earth can keep intercession out. **Richard Halverson**

I am as certain as I am standing here, that the secret of much mischief to our own souls, and to the souls of others, lies in the way that we stint, and starve, and scamp our prayers, by hurrying over them. **Alexander Whyte**

Prayer is the Lord's great sterilizer against the germs of spiritual disease. **James E. Talmage**

Every great movement of God can be traced to a kneeling figure. **Dwight L. Moody**

Prayer is no fitful, short-lived thing. It is no voice crying unheard and unheeded in the silence. It is a voice which goes into God's ear, and it lives as long as God's ear is open to holy pleas, as long as God's heart is alive to holy things. **Edward McKendree Bounds**

Nothing tends more to cement the hearts of Christians than praying together. Never do they love one another so well as when they witness the outpouring of each other's hearts in prayer. **Charles Grandison Finney**

Prayer is the way you defeat the devil, reach the lost, restore a backslider, strengthen the saints, send missionaries out, cure the sick, accomplish the impossible, and know the will of God. **David Jeremiah**

...True prayer is measured by weight, not by length. A single groan before God may have more fullness of prayer in it than a fine oration of great length. **Charles Spurgeon**

Is prayer your steering wheel or your spare tire? **Corrie Ten Boom**

A prayerless church member is a hindrance. He is in the body like a rotting bone or a decayed tooth. Before long, since he does not contribute to the benefit of his brethren, he will become a danger and a sorrow to them. Neglect of private prayer is the locust which devours the strength of the church. **Charles Spurgeon**

When the devil sees a man or woman who really believes in prayer, who knows how to pray, and who really does pray, and, above all, when he sees a whole church on its face before God in prayer, he trembles as much as he ever did, for he knows that his day in that church or community is at an end. **R. A. Torrey**

Prayer is not asking. Prayer is putting oneself in the hands of God, at His disposition, and listening to His voice in the depth of our hearts. **Mother Teresa**

We can be tired, weary and emotionally distraught, but after spending time alone with God, we find that He injects into our bodies energy, power and strength. **Charles Stanley**

The purpose of prayer is to reveal the presence of God equally present, all the time, in every condition. **Oswald Chambers**

Source:
https://www.azquotes.com/quotes/topics/prayer.html

The Bible on Prayer

In the previous section, we read some very inspirational sayings about prayer. As important as these may be, nothing can be more significant or impactful on our lives than the inspired Word of God. Let us therefore turn our attention to what the Bible has to say about prayer.

"Answer me when I call, O God of my righteousness! You have given me relief when I was in distress. Be gracious to me and hear my prayer!" **(Psalm 4:1)**

"Therefore let everyone who is godly offer prayer to you at a time when you may be found; surely in the rush of great waters, they shall not reach him." **(Psalm 32:6)**

Pathways to a Brighter Future

"Hear my prayer, O Lord, and give ear to my cry; hold not your peace at my tears! For I am a sojourner with you, a guest, like all my fathers." **(Psalm 39:12)**

"But truly God has listened; he has attended to the voice of my prayer." **(Psalm 66:19)**

"But as for me, my prayer is to you, O Lord. At an acceptable time, O God, in the abundance of your steadfast love answer me in your saving faithfulness." **(Psalm 69:13)**

"For the Lord builds up Zion; he appears in his glory; he regards the prayer of the destitute and does not despise their prayer." **(Psalm 102:16-17)**

"You will make your prayer to him, and he will hear you, and you will pay your vows." **(Job 22:27)**

"The Lord is far from the wicked, but he hears the prayer of the righteous." **(Proverbs 15:29)**

"Now therefore, O our God, listen to the prayer of your servant and to his pleas for mercy, and for your own sake, O Lord, make your face to shine upon your sanctuary, which is desolate." **(Daniel 9-17)**

"When my life was fainting away, I remembered the Lord, and my prayer came to you, into your holy temple." **(Jonah 2:7)**

"Therefore I tell you, whatever you ask in prayer, believe that you have received it, and it will be yours." **(Mark 11:24)**

HOPE

"I am praying for them. I am not praying for the world but for those whom you have given me, for they are yours." **(John 17:9)**

"Likewise the Spirit helps us in our weakness. For we do not know what to pray for as we ought, but the Spirit himself intercedes for us with groanings too deep for words." **(Romans 8:26)**

"Rejoice in hope, be patient in tribulation, be constant in prayer." **(Romans 12:12)**

"Let your reasonableness be known to everyone. The Lord is at hand; do not be anxious about anything, but in everything by prayer and supplication with thanksgiving let your requests be made known to God. And the peace of God, which surpasses all understanding, will guard your hearts and your minds in Christ Jesus." **(Philippians 4:5-7)**

"Continue steadfastly in prayer, being watchful in it with thanksgiving." **(Colossians 4:2)**

"In the days of his flesh, Jesus offered up prayers and supplications, with loud cries and tears, to him who was able to save him from death, and he was heard because of his reverence." **(Hebrews 5:7)**

"Is anyone among you suffering? Let him pray. Is anyone cheerful? Let him sing praise." **(James 5:13)**

"Therefore, confess your sins to one another and pray for one another, that you may be healed. The prayer of a righteous person has great power as it is working." **(James 5:16)**

"Beloved, I pray that all may go well with you and that you may be in good health, as it goes well with your soul." **(3 John 1:2)**

Lessons to be Learned

We can learn several lessons about prayer from the preceding verses. Among them are the following:

1. Jesus set an example by praying to the Father on His own bealf
2. Christ prayed for us, His followers
3. The Holy Spirit intercedes for us
4. We must be constant in prayer
5. We must make our requests known to God even though He knows our needs
6. We must offer prayers of thanksgiving
7. We must pray for one another; prayer has great power.
8. God always hears us when we pray.

The Model Prayer

Jesus spent much time in prayer. On one occasion, He was at a certain place praying. When He was finished praying, one of His disciples approached Him, asking Him to teach them to pray as John (the Baptist) taught his disciples. There must have been something peculiar about the way Jesus and John's disciples prayed that prompted such a request. In response, Jesus offered the following prayer which is now commonly known as the Lord's Prayer.

"After this manner therefore pray ye: Our Father which art in heaven, Hallowed be thy name.

Thy kingdom come, Thy will be done in earth, as it is in heaven.

Give us this day our daily bread.

And forgive us our debts, as we forgive our debtors.

And lead us not into temptation, but deliver us from evil: For thine is the kingdom, and the power, and the glory, for ever. Amen."

Let us give a brief analysis this model prayer. Note that the prayer is relatively short and to the point. It identifies the One to whom the prayer is made—the Holy Father in heaven. Next, there is a prayer for God's will to be done on earth as it is done in heaven (obedience and consecration). The prayer then proceeds to supplication by asking for our daily sustenance (bread). A plea for forgiveness follows, then an entreaty for protection.

Notable Pray-ers and Their Prayers in the Bible

In this section, we focus our attention on four notable pray-ers and their prayers. The pray-ers are:

Hannah

David

Solomon

Stephen

Pathways to a Brighter Future

Hannah

The story of Hannah is well-known to Bible scholars. Her husband, Elkanah, had another wife named Peninnah. Hannah was infertile while Peninnah had children. Peninnah provoked Hannah because of her infertility. This troubled Hannah greatly, so she prayed to God for a son. When God answered her prayer by giving her a son, Samuel the prophet, she offered the following prayer of praise and thanksgiving.

Hannah's Prayer

Then Hannah prayed and said:

"My heart rejoices in the LORD;
in the LORD my horn[a] is lifted high.
My mouth boasts over my enemies,
for I delight in your deliverance.

"There is no one holy like the LORD;
there is no one besides you;
there is no Rock like our God.

"Do not keep talking so proudly
or let your mouth speak such arrogance,
for the LORD is a God who knows,
and by him deeds are weighed.

"The bows of the warriors are broken,
but those who stumbled are armed with strength.
Those who were full hire themselves out for food,
but those who were hungry are hungry no more.
She who was barren has borne seven children,
but she who has had many sons pines away.

HOPE

*"The L*ORD *brings death and makes alive;*
he brings down to the grave and raises up.
*The L*ORD *sends poverty and wealth;*
he humbles and he exalts.
He raises the poor from the dust
and lifts the needy from the ash heap;
he seats them with princes
and has them inherit a throne of honor.

*"For the foundations of the earth are the L*ORD*'s;*
on them he has set the world.
He will guard the feet of his faithful servants,
but the wicked will be silenced in the place of darkness.

"It is not by strength that one prevails;
*those who oppose the L*ORD *will be broken.*
The Most High will thunder from heaven;
*the L*ORD *will judge the ends of the earth.*

"He will give strength to his king
and exalt the horn of his anointed."
1 Samuel 2:1-10

David

David was king of Israel. He lusted after Bathsheba, committed adultery with her, and murdered her husband. The following is his prayer of confession and repentance.

David's Prayer

Have mercy on me, O God,
according to your unfailing love;
according to your great compassion
blot out my transgressions.

Pathways to a Brighter Future

*Wash away all my iniquity
and cleanse me from my sin.*

*For I know my transgressions,
and my sin is always before me.
Against you, you only, have I sinned
and done what is evil in your sight;
so you are right in your verdict
and justified when you judge.
Surely I was sinful at birth,
sinful from the time my mother conceived me.
Yet you desired faithfulness even in the womb;
you taught me wisdom in that secret place.*

*Cleanse me with hyssop, and I will be clean;
wash me, and I will be whiter than snow.
Let me hear joy and gladness;
let the bones you have crushed rejoice.
Hide your face from my sins
and blot out all my iniquity.*

*Create in me a pure heart, O God,
and renew a steadfast spirit within me.
Do not cast me from your presence
or take your Holy Spirit from me.
Restore to me the joy of your salvation
and grant me a willing spirit, to sustain me.*

*Then I will teach transgressors your ways,
so that sinners will turn back to you.
Deliver me from the guilt of bloodshed, O God,
you who are God my Savior,
and my tongue will sing of your righteousness.
Open my lips, Lord,
and my mouth will declare your praise.
You do not delight in sacrifice, or I would bring it;*

you do not take pleasure in burnt offerings.
My sacrifice, O God, is[b] a broken spirit;
a broken and contrite heart
you, God, will not despise.

May it please you to prosper Zion,
to build up the walls of Jerusalem.
Then you will delight in the sacrifices of the righteous,
in burnt offerings offered whole;
then bulls will be offered on your altar.

Solomon

Solomon was king of Israel after his father, David. He is known for his wisdom. King David wanted to build a temple for the Lord, but God did not permit him. However, God permitted David's son, Solomon to build a temple. The following is Solomon's prayer at the dedication of the temple.

Solomon's Prayer

Then Solomon stood before the altar of the LORD in front of the whole assembly of Israel, spread out his hands toward heaven and said:

"LORD, the God of Israel, there is no God like you in heaven above or on earth below—you who keep your covenant of love with your servants who continue wholeheartedly in your way. You have kept your promise to your servant David my father; with your mouth you have promised and with your hand you have fulfilled it— as it is today.

"Now LORD, the God of Israel, keep for your servant David my father the promises you made to him when you said, 'You shall never fail to have a successor to sit before *me on the throne of Israel, if only your descendants are careful in all they do to walk before me faithfully as you have done.' And now, God of Israel, let your word that you promised your servant David my father come true.*

"But will God really dwell on earth? The heavens, even the highest heaven, cannot contain you. How much less this temple I have built! Yet give attention to your servant's prayer and his plea for mercy, LORD my God. Hear the cry and the prayer that your servant is praying in your presence this day. May your eyes be open toward this temple night and day, this place of which you said, 'My Name shall be there,' so that you will hear the prayer your servant prays toward this place. Hear the supplication of your servant and of your people Israel when they pray toward this place. Hear from heaven, your dwelling place, and when you hear, forgive.

"When anyone wrongs their neighbor and is required to take an oath and they come and swear the oath before your altar in this temple, then hear from heaven and act. Judge between your servants, condemning the guilty by bringing down on their heads what they have done, and vindicating the innocent by treating them in accordance with their innocence.

"When your people Israel have been defeated by an enemy because they have sinned against you, and when they turn back to you and give praise to your name, praying and making supplication to you in this temple, then hear from heaven and forgive the sin of your people Israel and bring them back to the land you gave to their ancestors.

"When the heavens are shut up and there is no rain because your people have sinned against you, and when they pray toward this place and give praise to your name and turn from their sin because you have afflicted

HOPE

them, then hear from heaven and forgive the sin of your servants, your people Israel. Teach them the right way to live, and send rain on the land you gave your people for an inheritance.

"When famine or plague comes to the land, or blight or mildew, locusts or grasshoppers, or when an enemy besieges them in any of their cities, whatever disaster or disease may come, and when a prayer or plea is made by anyone among your people Israel—being aware of the afflictions of their own hearts, and spreading out their hands toward this temple— then hear from heaven, your dwelling place. Forgive and act; deal with everyone according to all they do, since you know their hearts (for you alone know every human heart), so that they will fear you all the time they live in the land you gave our ancestors.

"As for the foreigner who does not belong to your people Israel but has come from a distant land because of your name— for they will hear of your great name and your mighty hand and your outstretched arm—when they come and pray toward this temple, then hear from heaven, your dwelling place. Do whatever the foreigner asks of you, so that all the peoples of the earth may know your name and fear you, as do your own people Israel, and may know that this house I have built bears your Name.

"When your people go to war against their enemies, wherever you send them, and when they pray to the L*ORD* *toward the city you have chosen and the temple I have built for your Name, then hear from heaven their prayer and their plea, and uphold their cause.*

"When they sin against you—for there is no one who does not sin—and you become angry with them and give them over to their enemies, who take them captive to their own lands, far away or near; and if they have a

change of heart in the land where they are held captive, and repent and plead with you in the land of their captors and say, 'We have sinned, we have done wrong, we have acted wickedly'; and if they turn back to you with all their heart and soul in the land of their enemies who took them captive, and pray to you toward the land you gave their ancestors, toward the city you have chosen and the temple I have built for your Name; then from heaven, your dwelling place, hear their prayer and their plea, and uphold their cause. And forgive your people, who have sinned against you; forgive all the offenses they have committed against you, and cause their captors to show them mercy; for they are your people and your inheritance, whom you brought out of Egypt, out of that iron-smelting furnace.

"May your eyes be open to your servant's plea and to the plea of your people Israel, and may you listen to them whenever they cry out to you. For you singled them out from all the nations of the world to be your own inheritance, just as you declared through your servant Moses when you, Sovereign LORD, *brought our ancestors out of Egypt."*

When Solomon had finished all these prayers and supplications to the LORD, *he rose from before the altar of the* LORD, *where he had been kneeling with his hands spread out toward heaven. He stood and blessed the whole assembly of Israel in a loud voice, saying:*

"Praise be to the LORD, *who has given rest to his people Israel just as he promised. Not one word has failed of all the good promises he gave through his servant Moses. May the* LORD *our God be with us as he was with our ancestors; may he never leave us nor forsake us. May he turn our hearts to him, to walk in obedience to him and keep the commands, decrees and laws he gave our ancestors. And may these words of mine, which I have*

*prayed before the L*ORD*, be near to the L*ORD *our God day and night, that he may uphold the cause of his servant and the cause of his people Israel according to each day's need, so that all the peoples of the earth may know that the L*ORD *is God and that there is no other. And may your hearts be fully committed to the L*ORD *our God, to live by his decrees and obey his commands, as at this time."*

Stephen

Stephen was chosen as one of the seven deacons of the early Christian Church in Jerusalem. The Bible describes him as a man full of faith and of the Holy Spirit. False accusations were brought against him, and while he was defending himself from the charges laid against him, his hearers became angry and stoned him to death. Just before his death, he offered the following prayer:

"Lord Jesus, receive my spirit."

Then he fell on his knees and cried out, *"Lord, do not hold this sin against them."*

The Power of Prayer

Prayer is a powerful weapon at our disposal. Through the power of prayer, infertility is cured (1 Samuel 1:11-20), prisoners are released from prison (Acts 12:5-9; 16:25, 26), and evil spirits are cast out (Mark 9:15-29). The following is a real-life story that demonstrates the power of prayer.

The young people from one church were invited to participate in a concert at another church. At the beginning of the concert, a young lady held a microphone to her mouth to offer the opening prayer, but it was non-functional. She tapped it and checked to make sure it was turned on. It was, but it was dead. She tried another microphone but the result was the same. At that moment, the young lady bowed her head, closed her eyes, and prayed to God that the system would work. She tapped the microphone again, and it worked. The sound system worked perfectly throughout the concert. After the concert, the system ceased to function. Such is the power of prayer.

Prayer is not a futile exercise. Prayer produces results. The following acronym encourages us to continue in prayer:

Pray

Until

Something

Happens

What if God does not answer? God always answers earnest prayers (Job 22:27). Sometimes He says **Yes**, sometimes He says **Wait**, and sometimes He says **No**. We can console ourselves with the assurance that God loves us and wants the best for us.

"If you then, who are evil, know how to give good gifts to your children, how much more will the heavenly Father give the Holy Spirit to those who ask him!" **(Luke 11:13)**

Hope and Prayer

A close relationship exists between hope and prayer. One can see this relationship even superficially. For example, Jonathan has hope that he will be accepted at university into the chemistry program. His Dad suggests to him that he pray about it. He agrees. Now, Jonathan's optimism has assumed an additional dimension. God is now in the picture. His optimistic expectation of being accepted into the program of his choice is now bolstered by a solemn request from God Almighty. Imagine the confidence that is being inspired in Jonathan.

On a deeper level, hope enables us to cling to the future amidst all the turmoil, confusion, tribulations, and trials that we face. Prayer allows us to place all these burdens on the omnipotent One, God, thus brightening our path along life's journey.

Prayer

Father in heaven, we thank You for helping us to understand the significance and importance of prayer. Father, we pray that You will help us to come to You boldly in prayer. We pray that through prayer, we will develop a closer relationship with you. We thank You for the work of the Holy Spirit in presenting our prayers to you. We pray in Jesus' name.

Amen

CHAPTER 9: WISDOM

God wants us to be wise.

For wisdom is protection just as money is protection, But the advantage of knowledge is that wisdom preserves the lives of its possessors **(Ecclesiastes 7:12)**.

This book is about having a good life now and everlasting life in the future. The decisions we make have significant effects on our lives now and in the future. In the same way that we reap the benefits of wise choices, so too we must face the consequences of bad decisions. We cannot expect to have a healthy life if we neglect to get sufficient sleep, fail to provide our bodies with necessary nutrients, neglect to exercise, and ignore proper hygiene. In this chapter, we pay some attention to the extremely important concept of wisdom.

What is Wisdom?

It is important that we have a clear understanding of the meaning of the word wisdom. In daily conversations, we use the word wisdom freely to refer to concepts such as education and knowledge. Although wisdom may be associated with education and knowledge, they are not identical concepts. You probably know people who are well educated and have numerous certificates, diplomas, and degrees to demonstrate their education, but who are not at all wise. Likewise, you probably know many people who know a great deal about a wide variety of things, but you probably wouldn't regard many of those as being wise.

Collins Dictionary defines wisdom as follows:

"Wisdom is the ability to use your experience and knowledge in order to make sensible decisions or judgments."

Clearly, according to this definition, one can have experience and knowledge without having wisdom. Apparently, wisdom is demonstrated by the nature of the decisions and judgments that one makes.

Wisdom versus Knowledge

We can probably get a deeper sense of the meaning of wisdom by considering the difference between wisdom and knowledge. Wisdom, as we have seen, is the ability to make wise decisions; the ability to use knowledge intelligently. Knowledge, on the other hand, is information about something or someone. It is an awareness of facts. The following quotation by an unknown author will help to clarify the difference between wisdom and knowledge:

"Knowledge is knowing what to say. Wisdom is knowing when to say it."

We can summarize this section by saying that wisdom is the prudent use of knowledge. You can have knowledge without wisdom, but you can't have wisdom without knowledge.

Sayings about Wisdom

We can learn much about a concept by what others have to say about it. Our understanding of wisdom will be broadened and deepened by reading what others have to say about it. Here are some statements about wisdom.

Wisdom comes with the ability to be still. Just look and just listen. No more is needed. Being still, looking, and listening activates the non-conceptual intelligence within you. Let stillness direct your words and actions. **Eckhart Tolle**

The wise man hath his thoughts in his head; the fool, on his tongue. **Ivan Panin**

An intelligent man believes only half of what he hears, a wise man knows which half. **Evan Esar**

The difference between a wise and foolish man is this--the former sees much, thinks much, and speaks little; but the latter speaks more than he either sees or thinks. **William Scott Downey**

Wisdom comes only through suffering. **Aeschylus**

HOPE

Wisdom is not communicable. The wisdom which a wise man tries to communicate always sounds foolish.... Knowledge can be communicated, but not wisdom. One can find it, live it, do wonders through it, but one cannot communicate and teach it. **Hermann Hesse**

Wisdom is understanding when to ask questions. **Brian Herbert & Kevin J. Anderson**

The kind of man who always thinks that he is right, that his opinions, his pronouncements, are the final word, when once exposed shows nothing there. But a wise man has much to learn without a loss of dignity. **Sophocles**

You may not have very much sense. But if you have enough to keep your mouth shut and look wise, it will not be long before you acquire a wide reputation as a fountain of Wisdom. **Robert Elliott Gonzales**

Be very slow to believe that you are wiser than all others; it is a fatal but common error. **Charles Caleb Colton**

Knowledge is flour, but wisdom is bread. **Austin O'malley**

Look about, my son, and see how little wisdom it takes to govern the world. **Axel Oxenstierna**

Wisdom is a treasure, the key whereof is never lost. **Edward Counsel**

Like water in the desert is wisdom to the soul. **Edward Counsel**

An ignorant man is always able to say yes or no immediately to any proposition. To a wise man, comparatively few things can be propounded which do not require a response with qualifications, with discriminations, with proportion. **Horace Mann**

It requires wisdom to understand wisdom: The music is nothing if the audience is deaf. **Walter Lippmann**

Wisdom is the daughter of experience. **Leonardo Da Vinci**

Wisdom is the reward you get for a lifetime of listening when you'd have preferred to talk. **Doug Larson**

Let men be wise by instinct if they can, but when this fails be wise by good advice. **Sophocles**

Fools talk, cowards are silent, wise men listen. **Carlos Ruiz Zafon**

Mixing one's wines may be a mistake, but old and new wisdom mix admirably.

Bertolt Brecht

True wisdom is knowing what you don't know. **Confucius**

Wise men are instructed by reason; men of less understanding, by experience; the most ignorant, by necessity; and beasts, by nature. **Cicero**

You know the difference between knowledge and wisdom? Knowledge is knowing tomato is a fruit. Wisdom is knowing you don't put tomato in a fruit salad. **Gene Kesselman**

There are many gates to the house of wisdom. **Edward Counsel**

Wisdom is the quality that keeps you from getting into situations where you need it. **Doug Larson**

Common sense in an uncommon degree is what the world calls wisdom.

Samuel Taylor Coleridge

Wisdom is ever fresh; other things grow stale, but this is the evergreen flower of nature. **Edward Counsel**

To understand the actual world as it is, not as we should wish it to be, is the beginning of wisdom. **Bertrand Russell**

Wisdom grows in quiet places. **Austin O'malley**

Wisdom is sold in the desolate market where none come to buy, And in the withered fields where the farmer ploughs for bread in vain.

William Blake

A wise man can learn more from a foolish question than a fool can learn from a wise answer. **Bruce Lee**

Knowledge is proud that he has learn'd so much; Wisdom is humble that he knows no more. **William Cowper**

Memory is the mother of all wisdom. **Aeschylus**

Source: http://www.notablequotes.com/w/wisdom_quotes_ii.html

Pathways to a Brighter Future

The Bible on Wisdom

According to Wikipedia*, there are 222 references in the Bible to wisdom. In the Bible, wisdom is presented as a virtue to be sought after and cherished. In this section, we reference numerous Bible texts that pertain to wisdom.

For the Lord gives wisdom; from his mouth come knowledge and understanding. **(Proverbs 2:6)**

Be very careful, then, how you live—not as unwise but as wise, making the most of every opportunity, because the days are evil. **(Ephesians 5:15-16)**

If any of you lacks wisdom, you should ask God, who gives generously to all without finding fault, and it will be given to you. **(James 1:5)**

But the wisdom that comes from heaven is first of all pure; then peace-loving, considerate, submissive, full of mercy and good fruit, impartial and sincere. **(James 3:17)**

How much better to get wisdom than gold, to get insight rather than silver! **(Proverbs 16:16)**

Do not say, "Why were the old days better than these?"
For it is not wise to ask such questions. **(Ecclesiastes 7:10)**

Source:
*https://en.wikipedia.org/wiki/Wisdom#:~:text=The%20word%20wisdom%20(%D7%97%D7%9B%D7%9D)%20is,and%20to%20increase%20in%20wisdom.

Be wise in the way you act toward outsiders; make the most of every opportunity. Let your conversation be

HOPE

always full of grace, seasoned with salt, so that you may know how to answer everyone. **(Colossians 4:5-6)**

Where there is strife, there is pride, but wisdom is found in those who take advice. **(Proverbs 13:10)**

The one who gets wisdom loves life; the one who cherishes understanding will soon prosper. **(Proverbs 19:8)**

Do not deceive yourselves. If any of you think you are wise by the standards of this age, you should become "fools" so that you may become wise. **(1 Corinthians 3:18)**

Who is wise and understanding among you? Let them show it by their good life, by deeds done in the humility that comes from wisdom. **(James 3:13)**

Therefore everyone who hears these words of mine and puts them into practice is like a wise man who built his house on the rock. **(Matthew 7:24)**

Teach us to number our days, that we may gain a heart of wisdom. **(Psalm 90:12)**

When pride comes, then comes disgrace, but with humility comes wisdom. **(Proverbs 11:2)**

Wisdom's instruction is to fear the Lord, and humility comes before honor. **(Proverbs 15:33)**

I keep asking that the God of our Lord Jesus Christ, the glorious Father, may give you the Spirit of wisdom and revelation, so that you may know him better. **(Ephesians 1:17)**

The wise in heart accept commands, but a chattering fool comes to ruin. **(Proverbs 10:8)**

Pathways to a Brighter Future

I thank and praise you, God of my ancestors: You have given me wisdom and power, you have made known to me what we asked of you, you have made known to us the dream of the king. **(Daniel 2:23)**

All this also comes from the Lord Almighty, whose plan is wonderful, whose wisdom is magnificent. **(Isaiah 28:29)**

Even fools are thought wise if they keep silent, and discerning if they hold their tongues. **(Proverbs 17:28)**

The beginning of wisdom is this: Get wisdom. Though it cost all you have, get understanding. **(Proverbs 4:7)**

For with much wisdom comes much sorrow; the more knowledge, the more grief. **(Ecclesiastes 1:18)**

Blessed are those who find wisdom, those who gain understanding. **(Proverbs 3:13)**

The fear of the Lord is the beginning of knowledge, but fools despise wisdom and instruction. **(Proverbs 1:7)**

The fear of the Lord is the beginning of wisdom, and knowledge of the Holy One is understanding. **(Proverbs 9:10)**

Know also that wisdom is like honey for you: If you find it, there is a future hope for you, and your hope will not be cut off. **(Proverbs 24:14)**

I instruct you in the way of wisdom and lead you along straight paths. **(Proverbs 4:11)**

HOPE

Oh, the depth of the riches of the wisdom and knowledge of God! How unsearchable his judgments, and his paths beyond tracing out! **(Romans 11:33)**

Get wisdom, get understanding; do not forget my words or turn away from them. **(Proverbs 4:5)**

Walk with the wise and become wise, for a companion of fools suffers harm. **(Proverbs 13:20)**

Words from the mouth of the wise are gracious, but fools are consumed by their own lips. **(Ecclesiastes 10:12)**

The fear of the Lord is the beginning of wisdom; all who follow his precepts have good understanding. To him belongs eternal praise. **(Psalm 111:10)**

My son, if your heart is wise, then my heart will be glad indeed. **(Proverbs 23:15)**

The law of the Lord is perfect, refreshing the soul. The statutes of the Lord are trustworthy, making wise the simple. **(Psalm 19:7)**

Fools give full vent to their rage, but the wise bring calm in the end. **(Proverbs 29:11)**

The father of a righteous child has great joy; a man who fathers a wise son rejoices in him. **(Proverbs 23:24)**

Many will be purified, made spotless and refined, but the wicked will continue to be wicked. None of the wicked will understand, but those who are wise will understand. **(Daniel 12:10)**

A wise son brings joy to his father, but a foolish son brings grief to his mother. **(Proverbs 10:1)**

Who is wise? Let them realize these things.
Who is discerning? Let them understand.
The ways of the Lord are right;
the righteous walk in them,
but the rebellious stumble in them. **(Hosea 14:9)**

Source: https://dailyverses.net/wisdom?p=3

The Benefits of Wisdom

The Bible admonishes us to seek wisdom because God, in his infinite wisdom, wants us to be wise. As disciples of Christ, we must be as wise as serpents and as harmless as doves (Matthew 10:16). People who are wise derive numerous benefits from their wisdom. Some of these benefits are analyzed below:

Benefits of Wisdom to the Individual

Better Decision-Making: The decisions that individuals make on a daily basis can have lasting effects on their lives. For example, the decision to join the labour force immediately after graduating from secondary school instead of pursuing tertiary education can significantly affect an individual's life short-term and long-term in terms of employment, income, and social interactions. With wisdom, the individual is able to make choices that are in alignment with his or her personal goals.

Enhanced Problem-Solving Skills: Problems are a permanent fixture of life at various stages, and the ability to solve various types of problems makes life more enjoyable. Wisdom enables individuals to anticipate challenges and to deal effectively with them before they develop into more serious problems. On the emotional side, effective problem-solving skills made possible through wisdom, relieve stress and contribute to emotional health.

Improved Interpersonal Relationships: It was John Donne who reminded us that "No man is an island entire of itself." We live in a world of interdependence, and the better we relate to others, the more meaningful our lives will be. Wisdom helps us to understand the actions and motives of others and thus enables us to develop better relationships with those with whom we come into contact. It enables us to resolve conflicts, thus promoting a more peaceful and harmonious environment.

Personal Growth and Development: It is safe to assume that most rational people desire personal growth and development. We want to be better versions of ourselves. Wisdom gives us the ability to perceive who and what we are, and the ability to discern what is needed to get us to where we want to be.

Increase in Wealth: A foolish lifestyle is characterized by recklessness, lawlessness, harmful practices, and generally little regard for wholesome living. This type of lifestyle is conducive to physical and mental illnesses with their concomitant costs. Wisdom causes the individual to shun a foolish lifestyle and thus save significant amounts of money which adds to wealth.

Personal Satisfaction: Wisdom enables us to say and do things that are helpful to others. For example, a family might be facing a crisis from which it sees no escape. Through your wisdom, you may be able to offer a suggestion that averts the crises. This brings joy and gladness to the family, and great personal satisfaction to you, knowing that you are able to help the family.

Benefits of Wisdom to the Society

The benefits of wisdom to society are also significant and pervasive. What follows below is but a small, illustrative sample of the benefits of wisdom to society.

Better Leadership: A society with wise individuals benefits from wisdom by having wise people from whom to choose as leaders. Social policies and political decisions can be guided by people who have insight and discernment. The judicial system, the educational system, the health system, the financial system, and the business sector will all benefit by having wise people in the society.

A More Cohesive Society: Wisdom results in a more cohesive society. It creates a feeling of unity and cohesion among the members of the society. It also fosters a sense of belonging. When people are able to reason together, seeing eye-to-eye, the entire society will be better off for it. Racism and other divisive elements will not flourish in a society where wisdom abounds.

Diminished Crime Rate: Crime severely diminishes the value of a society and inflicts unwanted costs on its members. Wisdom is likely to result in fewer violations of the law and a safer society in general.

Transfer of Knowledge from Generation to Generation: A society is enriched by the intergeneration of knowledge and culture. Much knowledge is lost owing to the failure of one generation to pass on knowledge, customs, and traditions to the future. Wisdom will prevent this loss.

Sustainable Development: Wisdom encourages a long-term perspective that prioritizes sustainable practices and responsible resource management. This leads to environmental conservation, reduced waste, and a focus on leaving a positive legacy for future generations.

To summarize, the benefits of wisdom to a society are multifaceted, spanning from better leadership, a more cohesive society, diminished crime rate, to a transfer of knowledge and sustainable development. As wisdom permeates the fabric of a community, it contributes to a more harmonious, equitable, and thriving society for all its members.

Hope and Wisdom

You may recall our discussion on false hope earlier in this book. We defined it as the emotion of confidence that something will happen when, in fact, it will not. As pointed out then, false hope has some undesirable consequences. Wisdom is a strong supporter of hope, but eliminates false hope. Indeed, hope and wisdom are closely connected. As we journey through life, we hope for certain conditions in the future. We know from Scripture that although all things are possible with God, with man, some things are impossible. Wisdom will help us to discern the things that are impossible with man. Wisdom prevents people from setting goals that are humanly unattainable by giving us a realistic understanding of the world. Hope provides us with the optimism to press onward amid life's tough challenges. Wisdom helps us to make the decisions that will achieve our goals.

Two Poems about Wisdom

The following two poems about wisdom highlight the value of that special virtue. Contemplate as you read them and focus on the central message: wisdom is to be sought after. In the first poem, the author pits wisdom against fame, power, and wealth—all desirable, but admonishes the youth to choose wisdom. The second poem points out what one ought to do if one is wise.

The Wise Choice

"Oh, give me fame!" a youth once cried
When touched by Fortune's wand,
"A fame that shines from shore to shore
And is known in every land,
And I will never ask again
Or seek more from thy hand."
Through years he grew and grew in fame
A lawyer great was he,
That wielded well the legal power
For gain and petty fee
Until bound down by greed of gain,
No longer was he free.

"Oh! give me power," an artist cried,
"To paint with steady hand
A picture that shall far excel
All others in the land,
And I shall have the riches all
That aught could e'er demand."
He painted then a picture true;
Folks marveled at the deed.
He soon won fame and wealth and power.
But, seized upon by greed,
All slipped away — power, wealth, and fame —
And left him sore in need.
"Oh! give me power to rule the land,
To sway affairs of state,
And I'll have wealth and power and fame,
And will be truly great,
And never, never will deplore

HOPE

Or wish to change my fate."
Time passed, and power was given him;
Of state he held the rein,
Until upon his conscience clear
Was left full many a stain,
For ah! so many deeds of shame
He did alone for gain.

"Oh! give me wealth, on every hand
To gain me thousand fold;
Take fame, take power, take honor all,
But give me yellow gold.
My heart will be as light and free
As was the gods of old."
Then wealth was given to the youth;
Without his least endeavor,
It quickly gained a thousandfold.
Wealth proved a powerful lever
That robbed the youth of honor bright
And doomed his soul forever.

"Oh! give me wisdom, grace, and peace,
A heart of purity,
An honest word that's always good
For any surety,
And I will always live content
Throughout futurity."
The youth was given wisdom grand
And purity of thought;
Then honor came, with fame and wealth
And glory all unsought.
Yet he despised the baser things,
For which the weaker sought.

O youth, choose wisdom while you may;
Let those who will choose pelf.
Contentment's yours with fame assured,
And these alone are wealth;

Pathways to a Brighter Future

While conscience clear will loud proclaim
You are an honor to yourself. **Lorain McLain**

If You Are Wise

If you are wise, you will forget yourself into greatness.
Forget your rights, but remember your responsibilities.
Forget your inconveniences, but remember your blessings.
Forget your own accomplishments, but remember your debts to others.
Forget your privileges, but remember your obligations.
Follow the examples of Florence Nightingale,
of Albert Schweitzer, of Abraham Lincoln, of Tom Dooley, and forget yourself into greatness.

If you are wise, you will empty yourself into adventure.
Remember the words of General Douglas MacArthur: "There is no security on this earth. There is only opportunity."
Empty your days of the search for security; fill them with a passion for service.
Empty your hours of the ambition for recognition; fill them with the aspiration for achievement.
Empty your moments of the need for entertainment; fill them with the quest for creativity.

If you are wise, you will lose yourself into immortality.
Lose your cynicism. Lose your doubts. Lose your fears.
Lose your anxiety. Lose your unbelief.
Remember these truths: A person must soon forget himself to be long remembered.
He must empty himself in order to discover a fuller self.
He must lose himself to find himself.
Forget yourself into greatness. Empty yourself into adventure. Lose yourself into immortality. **William Arthur Ward**

Prayer

Heavenly Father, You have invited us to ask for wisdom from you, so we are asking You, our Father, to endow us with wisdom from on high. We pray that You will help us to exercise wisdom in our daily decisions so that we can help others and make the community a better place to live.

Amen

Pathways to a Brighter Future

CHAPTER 10: HOPE AND RACISM

God's Word speaks out against racism. It is a pernicious blot on society

But if you show partiality, you are committing sin and are convicted by the law as transgressors (James 2:9)

Racism is a bane on society wherever it exists. It causes untold suffering and is responsible for societal disharmony and even death. The harmful effects of racism are well documented—poverty, poor psychological and physical health, poor quality of education, violence, physical and verbal abuse, to name a few. Racism is a deadly cancer eating away at the life of society. In this chapter, we will pay some attention to racism and its horrible effects. We will also examine the role of home in a racist environment.

Definition of Racism

Anyone who has ever experienced the disgust of racism knows exactly what racism is. However, for those readers who happen to be fortunate enough to escape its villainous tentacles, we will provide a definition here. The Oxford Dictionary defines prejudice as "discrimination, or antagonism by an individual, community, or institution against a person or people on the basis of their membership of a particular racial or ethnic group, typically one that is a minority or marginalized."

Does Racism Still Exist?

The answer to this question is a resounding yes. The origin of racism need not detain us here. Suffice it to say that it is not a new experience. However, it may be surprising to know that in our modern enlightened society, racism is still flourishing. Racism on any level is to be decried, but it is particularly dangerous when it is institutionalized. Institutionalized racism can find expression in ways such as persecution, ethnic cleansing, and legalized discrimination, and other such atrocities.

Evidence of Racism in Society

It is not difficult to see evidence of racism in our society. The following are some examples of racism:

- The unwillingness or refusal of landlords to rent their apartments to people of a certain race;
- The practice among employers to be hesitant to hire employees of a certain race;
- The inability of members of a certain race to earn wages commensurate with wages earned by others with similar qualifications for similar work;
- The difficulty experienced by some racial communities to get admission into certain social clubs or educational institutions;
- The unfair and unjust treatment by the law of members of a certain race;
- The persistence of families of a certain colour living in abject poverty because of prejudicial treatment by others, and
- Offenders being given much stiffer sentences by courts on the basis of their race.

Racial slurs

One way to judge the extent to which racism has dug its tentacles into society is by considering the extent to which the society uses racial slurs. Racial slurs are words or phrases that refer to members of racial and ethnic groups in a derogatory manner. The following table consists of a set of slurs and the targeted group.

Slur	Target
Coloured	A person who has black or brown skin
Coolie	A worker with no special skills in China, India, and other parts of Asia
Dago	A person from Italy, Spain, Portugal, or South America
Eskimo	A member of the Inuit people
Feringhee	Someone from a foreign country, especially a white person
Frog	A French person

HOPE

Gook	Someone from Asia
Gringo	Someone from the United States who speaks English
Half-breed	Someone who has parents of two different races
Half-caste	Someone with one black and one white parent
Honky	A white person
Mick	An Irish person
Mulatto	Someone with one whiye and one black parent
Nigger	A black person
Paddy	An Irish person
Paki	A South Asian person
Red Indian	A Native American
Redskin	A Native American
Spade	A black person
Squaw	A Native American woman
Taffy	Someone from Wales
Uncle Tom	A black person who is believed to show too much respect for white people
Wetback	Someone from Mexico who goes to live in the United States
Whitey	A white person
Wog	A person with black or brown skin; a person from a Mediterranean country
Wop	An Italian person
Yid	A Jewish person

Source: https://www.macmillandictionary.com/thesaurus-category/british/offensive-words-for-people-according-to-nationality-or-ethnicity

The Bible on Racism

It is interesting how some people who couldn't care less about what the Bible says about most other issues, and who otherwise view the Bible as "just an old story book" or a book of fairy tales, can use the same Bible to justify racism. It should be noted that there is not a single Bible text, interpreted correctly, that supports racism. On the contrary, as we demonstrate in this section, there are several Bible verses that warn against racism. This should not be surprising since the Bible teaches that we are all one in Christ.

The rich and the poor have a common bond, The LORD is the maker of them all. **(Proverbs 22:2).**

These also are sayings of the wise. To show partiality in judgment is not good. **(Proverbs 24:23).**

And he said to them, "You yourselves know how unlawful it is for a man who is a Jew to associate with a foreigner or to visit him; and yet God has shown me that I should not call any man unholy or unclean **(Acts 10:28).**

For there is no distinction between Jew and Greek; for the same Lord is Lord of all, abounding in riches for all who call on Him; for "WHOEVER WILL CALL ON THE NAME OF THE LORD WILL BE SAVED." **(Romans 10:12-13).**

There is neither Jew nor Greek, there is neither slave nor free man, there is neither male nor female; for you are all one in Christ Jesus **(Galatians 3:28).**

Here there is no Gentile or Jew, circumcised or uncircumcised, barbarian, Scythian, slave or free, but Christ is all, and is in all **(Colossians 3:11).**

But if you show partiality, you are committing sin and are convicted by the law as transgressors **(James 2:9)**.

But the one who hates his brother is in the darkness and walks in the darkness, and does not know where he is going because the darkness has blinded his eyes **(1 John 2:11)**.

The Effects of Racism on Society

In a racist society, all citizens are not given equal opportunities to participate in the development of the society, thus racism limits the potential of the racialized society. Because of racism, a society might deprive itself of developing great leaders in medicine, education, business, economics, and government. The suppression of any race will eventually lead to societal stagnation, aggression, and violence. At its worst, racism can lead to severe conflicts, riots, and even civil war. Racism prevents society from functioning optimally and if allowed to flourish, can lead to atrocities such as ethnic cleansing and genocide.

The Effects of Racism on the Individual

If someone is constantly told that he or she is worth less than other members of society, solely on the basis of race, he or she will begin to question himself/herself, and will eventually develop low self-esteem issues. Individuals against whom racism has been perpetrated develop feelings of resentment and hatred towards the perpetrators. They may turn to violence and criminal activities as a means of fighting back and lashing out on injustice.

The negative impact of racism on individuals is well documented. For example, psychotherapist Phillip Glickman has this to say:

"Racism negatively impacts the health and wellbeing of people of color. It can cause stress, anxiety, and depression. For example, high school students exposed to racism are at a higher risk of dropping out. Adolescents exposed to racism report higher rates of depressed mood. When surveyed, black teens reported facing racist actions five times a day on average. What's more, overt racism and hate crimes are on the rise on college campuses.

Exposure to racism can impact your self-esteem, cause you to feel helpless, and generate depression. Racism can impact other aspects of your health, raising the risk for heart disease, and gastrointestinal issues among others."

Source: https://www.wellnessroadpsychology.com/blog/depression-anxiety-and-how-racism-affects-people-of-color-and-non-poc

Clearly, racism is not something to encourage.

How to Develop Racial Harmony

Racial harmony exists when people of different races respect each other, and accept and promote the peaceful interaction and existence of all. We have seen that racism can wreak havoc on the individual and on the society at large. Racial harmony can prevent racism from taking root and spreading its dangerous tentacles in our society. Racism can be denounced by the relevant authorities in the workplace, in the media, in our schools, and in our communities. As individuals, we can do our part in developing racial harmony.

Here are some ways whereby we as individuals, can fight racism and develop racial harmony.

1. If you have been the perpetrator of racism, make a serious commitment to discontinue the practice. If you have been practicing it for a long time, it may be difficult to stop, but believe in yourself that you can do it.
2. Make a concerted effort to learn about races other than your own. Racism is due in large part to ignorance about other cultures and races.
3. Stand ready to make suggestions that will improve race relations at work. Do so in a spirit of cordiality.
4. Have the courage to speak up against the use of racial slurs and gestures that indicate racial prejudice. Do so in a manner that is unlikely to infuriate the perpetrator.
5. Racism is a learnt behavior. Help your children, if you are a parent, to become knowledgeable about races other than their own. Teach them, in an age-appropriate manner, that racism is wrong and that it is hurtful.

If we can successfully cultivate in our young people a feeling of tolerance and understanding of people who are different from their own race, then we can entertain hope of racial harmony in the future.

Hope and Racism

We have been discussing racism, its effects on society and the individual, and what can be done to develop racial harmony. Indeed, racism is a pernicious blot on society. In this final section of this chapter, we shall examine the role of hope in coping with racism. Horrible things like severe accidents, illnesses, tragedies of various types, racism, and sudden deaths are things that plague our neighbourhoods, our communities, our societies, our nations, and our world. Hear what the following poem has to say about hope and racism.

When racism raises its ugly head, hope tells us that we can move forward.

When racism threatens to keep us in bed in the mornings, hope gives us a reason to get out of bed.

When racism tries to convince us to give up the fight, hope gives us the assurance of final victory.

When racism seems to be gaining an upper hand, hope promises that we will overcome at last.

When racism causes us to be depressed and suicidal, hope enables us to see a brighter tomorrow.

Where racism tends to crush the human spirit, hope promises improved quality of life, self-esteem, and a sense of direction.

Whereas racism leads to helplessness and inadequacy, hope leads to resilience and perseverance. *E. M. James*

Prayer

God of mercy, God of love, hear us from Your throne above. You created us in Your image and crowned us with glory and honour. But Father, we have fallen far from Your ideal for us. Father, we pray that you will help us to understand that we are all Your children and that we are potential citizens of Your kingdom. We pray for racial harmony in our society, in Jesus' name. Amen

CHAPTER 11: SATAN AND HOPE

Satan is evil personified. He is a liar and a deceiver, and his objective is to destroy us.

Be alert and of sober mind. Your enemy the devil prowls around like a roaring lion looking for someone to devour. (1 Peter 5:8)

If you are at war, the more you know about your enemy, the better will be your chances of winning the war. Well, the truth is, whether you believe it or not, you are in a war with Satan, the enemy of God, and the more you know about him and his tactics, the better are your chances of defeating him in this cosmic conflict. In this chapter, you will learn about Satan, his army, his objectives, his strategies, the result of the cosmic conflict, and the role of hope in the conflict.

Satan

Who exactly is Satan? Our knowledge of Satan comes from the Holy Bible. We first encounter him in the Garden of Eden as a wise serpent in a conversation with Eve. The Bible describes Satan as "more crafty" than any of the wild animals the LORD God had made. Let us pick up the narrative in Genesis Chapter 3:

Serpent (Satan) to Eve: Did God really say, 'You must not eat from any tree in the garden'?"

Eve: We may eat fruit from the trees in the garden, but God did say, "You must not eat fruit from the tree that is in the middle of the garden, and you must not touch it, or you will die."

Satan: You will not certainly die, For God knows that when you eat from it your eyes will be opened, and you will be like God, knowing good and evil.

When the woman saw that the fruit of the tree was good for food and pleasing to the eye, and also desirable for gaining wisdom, she took some and ate it. She also gave some to her husband, who was with her, and he ate it. Then the eyes of both of them were opened, and they realized they were naked; so they sewed fig leaves together and made coverings for themselves.

Then the man and his wife heard the sound of the LORD God as he was walking in the garden in the cool of the day, and they hid from the LORD God among the trees of the garden. But the LORD God called to the man:

God (to Adam): Where are you?

Adam: I heard you in the garden, and I was afraid because I was naked; so I hid.

God: Who told you that you were naked? Have you eaten from the tree that I commanded you not to eat from?

Adam: The woman you put here with me—she gave me some fruit from the tree, and I ate it.

God (to Eve): What is this you have done?

Eve: The serpent deceived me, and I ate.

God (to Satan): Because you have done this, Cursed are you above all livestock and all wild animals! You will crawl on your belly and you will eat dust all the days of your life.

What can we learn from this episode about Satan? We learn that:

(1) Satan is cunning. His approach to Eve was to create doubt in her mind. "Did God really say …?"

(2) Satan is a deceiver. "The serpent deceived me…"

(3) Satan is a liar and an adversary of God. "You will not certainly die."

(4) Satan orchestrated the Fall of mankind.

Other Names for Satan

Since Satan (the Devil) is mentioned numerous times in Scripture, it is well that we know some of the other names by which he is called so that we can easily identify him. In the table below, we provide different names that are given in Scripture for Satan with their associated texts. Although several texts may use the same name for Satan, we quote only one text for each name. It should be noted that our list is by no means exhaustive, but it does give a good sample of alternative names for Satan. All the names by which Satan is known reveal certain aspects of his character. Tempter, Ruler of Demons, The Evil One, Liar, Adversary, Dragon, etc. are titles that warn us to beware of the creature who bears these names.

Names for Satan	Bible texts
Day-star, Son of the morning	How you are fallen from heaven, O day-star, son of the morning! how you are cut down to the ground, that did lay low the nations! (Isaiah 14:12).
Anointed Cherub	You were the anointed cherub that covered... (Ezekiel 28:14).
The Devil	Then Jesus was led up by the Spirit into the wilderness to be tempted by the Devil (Matthew 4:1).
Tempter	The tempter came and said to Him, "If You are the Son of God, command these stones to become loaves of bread" (Matthew 4:3).
Ruler of Demons	But the Pharisees said, "By the ruler of the demons He drives out demons" (Matthew 9:34).
Beelzebul	But when the Pharisees heard it, they said, "It is only by Beelzebul, the ruler of the demons, that this fellow casts out the demons" (Matthew 12:24).
The Evil One	When anyone hears the word of the kingdom and does not understand it, the evil one comes and snatches away what

HOPE

	is sown in the heart; this is what was sown on the path (Matthew 13:19).
Liar	You are of your father the Devil . . . there is no truth in him. When he speaks a lie, he speaks of his own nature: for he is a liar, and the father thereof (John 8:44).
Angel of Light	And no marvel; for even Satan fashions himself into an angel of light (2 Corinthians 11:14).
Belial	What agreement does Christ have with Belial? Or what does a believer share with an unbeliever? (2 Corinthians 6:15).
Adversary	Be sober, be watchful: your adversary the Devil, as a roaring lion, walks about, seeking whom he may devour (1 Peter 5:8).
Dragon	And the great dragon was cast down, the old serpent, he that is called the Devil and Satan, the deceiver of the whole world; he was cast down to the earth, and his angels were cast down with him (Revelation 12:9).
Lucifer	How art thou fallen from heaven, O Lucifer, son of the morning! how art thou cut down to the ground, which didst weaken the nations!
Day-star, Son of the morning	How you are fallen from heaven, O day-star, son of the morning! how you are cut down to the ground, that did lay low the nations! (Isaiah 14:12).

Source:
ttps://www.blueletterbible.org/faq/don_stewart/don_stewart_80.cfm

Satan's Army

This cosmic conflict is serious warfare. Make no mistakes about it. The stakes are high. The outcome of this war is known. Christ wins, Satan loses. The account is given in the final book of the Bible:

Then I saw the beast and the kings of the earth and their armies gathered together to wage war against the rider on the horse and his army. But the beast was captured, and with it the false prophet who had performed the signs on its behalf. With these signs he had deluded those who had received the mark of the beast and worshiped its image. The two of them were thrown alive into the fiery lake of burning sulfur. The rest were killed with the sword coming out of the mouth of the rider on the horse, and all the birds gorged themselves on their flesh. (Revelation 19:19-21).

This account is further supported by the following statement:

And the devil who had deceived them was cast into the lake of fire and brimstone, where the beast and the false prophet are; and they shall be tormented day and night for ever and ever. (Revelation 20:10).

Satan's army consists of the Devil himself as the leader, and approximately 33% of the angels in heaven whom he deceived and were cast out of heaven with him. His defeat is recorded as follows:

And there was war in heaven: Michael and his angels fought against the dragon; and the dragon fought and his angels, And prevailed not; neither was their place found any more in heaven. And the great dragon was cast out, that old serpent, called the Devil, and Satan, which deceiveth the whole world: he was cast out into the earth, and his angels were cast out with him. (Revelation 12:7-9).

In addition to the angels who were cast out of heaven with Satan, members of his army include people who align themselves with him by forsaking God. Satan is our enemy, and he does not want us to inherit the kingdom that Jesus has gone to prepare for us. So his tactic is to tempt human beings to disobey God's laws. If you forsake God and cling to Satan, you are a member of his army. Matthew 12:30 says, "Whoever is not with me is against me...."

Satan's Objectives and Strategies

Any leader who is worthy of the name must have goals and objectives, and must have strategies with which to achieve those goals. Knowing what those goals and strategies are, places us in a position to frustrate them and ultimately to defeat them.

Satan's Ultimate Goal

The Bible tells us that Satan's ultimate aim is to destroy us:

Be alert and of sober mind. Your enemy the devil prowls around like a roaring lion looking for someone to devour. **(1 Peter 5:8)**

And again, Simon, Simon, Satan has asked to sift all of you as wheat. **(Luke 22:31)**

This means that Satan desires to shake us so vigorously that we will not be able to stand firm. He wants to win us over to his side, but through faith in Christ and the blessed hope, we will be able to stand.

Satan's Strategies

Satan is a master strategist, and he will do whatever it takes to accomplish his evil intents, but Jesus will win the final conflict. The following table summarizes just a few of the strategies in Satan's arsenal. Don't forget that he is extremely cunning. To engage him in battle and to be victorious, we must:

"Put on the full armor of God, so that you can take your stand against the devil's schemes. For our struggle is not against flesh and blood, but against the rulers, against the authorities, against the powers of this dark world and against the spiritual forces of evil in the heavenly realms. Therefore put on the full armor of God, so that when the day of evil comes, you may be able to stand your ground, and after you have done everything, to stand. Stand firm then, with the belt of truth buckled around your waist, with the breastplate of righteousness in place, and with your feet fitted with the readiness that comes from the gospel of peace. In addition to all this, take up the shield of faith, with which you can extinguish all the flaming arrows of the evil one. Take the helmet of salvation and the sword of the Spirit, which is the word of God. (Ephesians 6:11-17)

Strategies	Bible text
Lies	...for he is a liar, and the father of it. (John 8:44)
Fear of death	and free those who all their lives were held in slavery by their fear of death. (Hebrews 2:15)
Misuse of scripture	For it is written: 'He will command his angels concerning you,...' (Matthew 4:6)
Signs and wonders	Even him, whose coming is after the working of Satan with all power and

	signs and lying wonders (2 Thessalonians 2:9)
Pride	... lest being lifted up with pride he fall into the condemnation of the devil. (1 Timothy 3:6)
Sex	Do not deprive one another, except perhaps by agreement for a limited time, that you may devote yourselves to prayer; but then come together again, so that Satan may not tempt you because of your lack of self-control. (1 Corinthians 7:5)
Anger	In your anger do not sin: Do not let the sun go down while you are still angry, and do not give the devil a foothold. (Ephesians 4:26, 27)
Opposition to God's word	God says, "You will die." Satan counters, "You will not certainly die." (Genesis 3:3,4)
Attack on faith	For this reason, when I could stand it no longer, I sent to find out about your faith. I was afraid that in some way the tempter had tempted you and that our labors might have been in vain. (1Thesalonians 3:5)
Exploitation of ignorance	When anyone hears the message about the kingdom and does not understand it, the evil one comes and snatches away what was sown in their heart... (Matthew 13:19).
Strategies	Bible text
Lies	...for he is a liar, and the father of it. (John 8:44)
Fear of death	and free those who all their lives were held in slavery by their fear of death. (Hebrews 2:15)

Pathways to a Brighter Future

Misuse of scripture	For it is written: 'He will command his angels concerning you,...' (Matthew 4:6)
Signs and wonders	Even him, whose coming is after the working of Satan with all power and signs and lying wonders (2 Thessalonians 2:9)
Pride	... lest being lifted up with pride he fall into the condemnation of the devil. (1 Timothy 3:6)
Sex	Do not deprive one another, except perhaps by agreement for a limited time, that you may devote yourselves to prayer; but then come together again, so that Satan may not tempt you because of your lack of self-control. (1 Corinthians 7:5)
Anger	In your anger do not sin: Do not let the sun go down while you are still angry, and do not give the devil a foothold. (Ephesians 4:26, 27)
Opposition to God's word	God says, "You will die." Satan counters, "You will not certainly die." (Genesis 3:3,4)
Attack on faith	For this reason, when I could stand it no longer, I sent to find out about your faith. I was afraid that in some way the tempter had tempted you and that our labors might have been in vain. (1Thesalonians 3:5)
Exploitation of ignorance	When anyone hears the message about the kingdom and does not understand it, the evil one comes and snatches away what was sown in their heart... (Matthew 13:19).
Strategies	Bible text
Lies	...for he is a liar, and the father of it. (John 8:44)

The Outcome of the Cosmic Conflict

We have already indicated that the High King of heaven, Jehovah God, will win this Great Controversy—this cosmic conflict between God and Satan. In the passage below, not only are the winner and loser identified, but the final doom of the loser is also indicated. Satan will be imprisoned for 1,000 years.

When the 1,000 years are finished, Satan will be free to leave his prison. He will go out and fool the nations who are over all the world. They are Gog and Magog. He will gather them all together for war. There will be as many as the sand along the sea-shore. They will spread out over the earth and all around the place where God's people are and around the city that is loved. Fire will come down from God out of heaven and destroy them. And the devil who deceived them was thrown into the lake of fire and brimstone, where the beast and the false prophet are also; and they will be tormented day and night forever and ever. **(Revelation 20:7-10)**

Hope and the Cosmic Conflict

In this great controversy, a time of persecution will come. The Bible describes it as "great tribulation, such as was not since the beginning of the world to this time, no, nor ever shall be." (Matthew 24:21). But hope will enable us to withstand anything that the devil and his followers will hurl at us. Hope strengthens us to resist Satan's lies, deceptions, and his attack on our faith. The assurance that the tribulation will end makes it easier to endure it. We will endure because we have this hope:

And then shall appear the sign of the Son of man in heaven: and then shall all the tribes of the earth mourn, and they shall see the Son of man coming in the clouds of heaven with power and great glory. And he shall send his angels with a great sound of a trumpet, and they shall gather together his elect from the four winds, from one end of heaven to the other. **(Matthew 24:30, 31).**

We have this hope that Christ is coming soon. Therefore we will persevere. We will hold on. We will not allow anyone to steal our crown.

Prayer

We thank you, Heavenly Father, for the truth revealed in this chapter. We believe that Satan is our adversary. We believe that he is a liar and a deceiver. We thank you, Father, for revealing to us his true identity and objective. We pray, dear God, that You will protect us from his wiles and deliver us from his tactics and strategies. This we ask in Jesus' Holy name.

Amen

HOPE

CHAPTER 12: BAPTISM

Baptism is a public demonstration that the person being baptized has decided to follow Jesus.

Whoever believes and is baptized will be saved, but whoever does not believe will be condemned **(Mark 16:16).**

Many Christian denominations practice baptism in one form or another to establish membership. You become a member of such churches by being baptized. In this chapter, we discuss the meaning and purpose of baptism, the different forms in practice, and what the Bible teaches about it. We begin with a definition of baptism.

The Definition of Baptism

Baptism means different things to different people. In all cases, however, it has something to do with water and is regarded as a religious practice. For purposes of this discussion, we define baptism as follows:

Baptism is the Christian ritual of immersing someone in water. It is a way of achieving membership into a church.

It is important to note that the Bible does not teach baptism by sprinkling, but rather by immersion.

Baptism versus Christening

Many people use the terms baptism and christening interchangeably. In this book, we use baptism and christening to refer to different concepts. As we have indicated earlier, baptism involves full immersion and is a public declaration that the individual has abandoned a sinful life and decided to adopt a Christian lifestyle. Christening as used in this book, refers to the sprinkling of water on an infant's forehead at the naming of the infant. The baptizing of infants cannot be justified since they cannot make a conscious decision to forsake a sinful life and walk in newness of life.

The Significance of Baptism

Baptism is an integral part of the life of someone who has forsaken a life of sin and who has decided to be a follower of Christ. Before we delve further into the significance of baptism, let us pause briefly to point out what baptism does not do. Whether you are baptized in the River Jordan, or in the Caribbean Sea, or in a pool in the vicinity of your church, baptism does not wash away your sins. Only the blood of Jesus can wash away you sin. We share the sentiments expressed by the following song:

What can wash away my sin?
Nothing but the blood of Jesus.
What can make me whole again?
Nothing but the blood of Jesus.
O precious is the flow
that makes me white as snow;
no other fount I know;
nothing but the blood of Jesus. **(Robert Lowry)**

For many believers, the motion of baptism which involves submersion (underwater) and rising symbolizes the burial (full submersion) and resurrection (rising up) of Jesus Christ. It is a public demonstration that you have decided to follow Jesus. Baptism is an open declaration of the symbolic death and burial of the old you, and the rising of the new creature to walk in the newness of life with Christ.

Bible Verses about Baptism

There is no shortage of Bible texts about baptism. Reviewing some of these verses will clarify our understanding of the subject and highlight its importance in the lives of Christians.

And Peter said to them, "Repent and be baptized every one of you in the name of Jesus Christ for the forgiveness of your sins, and you will receive the gift of the Holy Spirit. **(Acts 2:38)**

And now why do you wait? Rise and be baptized and wash away your sins, calling on his name.' **(Acts 22:16)**

Baptism, which corresponds to this, now saves you, not as a removal of dirt from the body but as an appeal to God for a good conscience, through the resurrection of Jesus Christ, **(1 Peter 3:21)**

Whoever believes and is baptized will be saved, but whoever does not believe will be condemned. **(Mark 16:16)**

Go therefore and make disciples of all nations, baptizing them in the name of the Father and of the Son and of the Holy Spirit, **(Matthew 28:19)**

Do you not know that all of us who have been baptized into Christ Jesus were baptized into his death? We were buried therefore with him by baptism into death, in order that, just as Christ was raised from the dead by the glory of the Father, we too might walk in newness of life. **(Romans 6:3-4)**

For as many of you as were baptized into Christ have put on Christ. **(Galatians 3:27)**

So those who received his word were baptized, and there were added that day about three thousand souls. **(Acts 2:41)**

And when Jesus was baptized, immediately he went up from the water, and behold, the heavens were opened to him, and he saw the Spirit of God descending like a dove and coming to rest on him; **(Matthew 3:16)**

And he commanded the chariot to stop, and they both went down into the water, Philip and the eunuch, and he baptized him. **(Acts 8:38)**

And he commanded them to be baptized in the name of Jesus Christ. Then they asked him to remain for some days. **(Acts 10:48)**

But when they believed Philip as he preached good news about the kingdom of God and the name of Jesus Christ, they were baptized, both men and women. **(Acts 8:12)**

"Can anyone withhold water for baptizing these people, who have received the Holy Spirit just as we have?" **(Acts 10:47)**

John appeared, baptizing in the wilderness and proclaiming a baptism of repentance for the forgiveness of sins. **(Mark 1:4)**

Special Note

It appears from some passages of Scripture (e.g., Acts 2:38 and 1 Peter 3:21) that the rite of baptism is necessary for salvation. The approach that we have taken in this book is that belief in the Lord Jesus Christ is the necessary and sufficient condition for salvation. Baptism, Sabbath-keeping, fellowshipping together, and communion are among the practices of Christians. They do them in obedience to God's commands because they are saved, not in order to be saved.

Sayings about Baptism

In this section, we take a look at what others have to say about baptism. Reading what others have to say about baptism gives us a broader perspective from which to view the topic. It may throw new light on the subject.

"From what cause the rite of baptism first proceeded is not expressed formally in the scripture, but it may be probably thought to be an imitation of the law of Moses concerning leprosy, wherein the leprous man was commanded to be kept out of the camp of Israel for a certain time, after which time being judged by the priest to be clean, he was admitted into the camp after a solemn washing. And this may therefore be a type of the washing in baptism, wherein such men as are cleansed of the leprosy of Sin by Faith, are received into the church with the solemnity of baptism." **(Thomas Hobbes)**

"Lastly, we must also know what Baptism signifies, and why God has ordained just such external sign and ceremony for the Sacrament by which we are first received into the Christian Church. But the act or ceremony is this, that we are sunk under the water, which passes over us, and afterwards are drawn out again. These two parts, to be sunk under the water and drawn out again, signify the power and operation of Baptism, which is nothing else than putting to death the old Adam, and after that the resurrection of the new man, both of which must take place in us all our lives, so that a truly Christian life is nothing else than a daily baptism, once begun and ever to be continued." **(Martin Luther)**

"Infant baptism when practiced can be no more than an expression of the faith and hope of the parents that their child will ultimately be saved." **(Lewis Sperry Chafer)**

"God's people should be baptized because God commanded it, not because some church requires it." **(John R. Rice)**

"Baptism is the catalyst to spiritual maturity, not the sign of having attained it." **(J.D. Greer)**

"Baptism is like the pool of Siloam, appointed for healing: it is salutary and medicinal: but the Spirit of God is that great angel that descends thither, and makes them virtual." **(Jeremy Taylor)**

"Baptism is rich in meaning. It suggests cleansing. When you are a disciple, you understand that you are cleansed by Christ. You understand that Christ died in your place on the cross, paying for your sins, fully forgiving you for all your wrongs. You are cleansed from guilt, and you are becoming a cleaner, healthier, more whole person." **(Brian D. Mclaren)**

"Baptism is like a precious jewel. Set apart by itself, it is nice and appealing but has nothing within it to compel. But place baptism against the backdrop of our sin and turn on the light of the cross and the jewel explodes with significance." **(John Mark Hicks)**

"The Church does not dispense the sacrament of baptism in order to acquire for herself an increase in membership but in order to consecrate a human being to God and to communicate to that person the divine gift of birth from God." **(Hans Urs Von Balthasar)**

"Baptism is, in fact, much more than a ritual conferring membership in a community, as many people conceive it nowadays. It is a process of birth, through which a new dimension of life opens out." **(Peter Seewald)**

"Rationally considered, nothing can be more absurd than the baptism of infants under any circumstances. No statement, no matter by whom it may be said to have been uttered, can make that true which is radically false. If an innocent child, unconscious of good or evil, irresponsible to God and man, incapable of thought or action, is not already, in accordance with Christian theology, a member of Christ, then no vicarious promise or priestly ablution can make him one. For if this were so, a similar ceremony under devil worship could make him a member of Satan." **(Tennessee Claflin)**

"Our justification from sins takes place at the point of saving faith, not at the point of water baptism, which usually occurs later. But if a person is already justified and has sins forgiven eternally at the point of saving faith, then baptism is not necessary for forgiveness of sins nor for the bestowal of new spiritual life. Baptism, then, is not necessary for salvation. But it is necessary if we are to be obedient to Christ, for he commanded baptism for all who believe in him." **(Wayne A. Grudem)**

"A funeral is not death, any more than baptism is birth or marriage union. All three are the clumsy devices, coming now too late, now too early, by which Society would register the quick motions of man." **(E.M. Forster)**

"In effect, baptism in New Testament theology is a loyalty oath, a public avowal of who is on the Lord's side in the cosmic war between good and evil." **(Michael S. Heiser)**

"Speaking of church membership without baptism is like speaking of marriage without vows: such a thing does not actually exist." **(Bobby Jamieson)**

HOPE

"It is impossible to enumerate how thoroughly Catholicism today is saturated by middle-class reasonableness; one need only recall how even baptism--once the most powerful expression of the church's opposition to the state, a symbol of entry into a spiritual countercommunity, a mystical adoption, less the bearing of a name than being led by means of a name on the first steps of one's inner way--is today bound up with middle-class record-keeping." **(Robert Musil)**

"Thus the vocation of the baptized person is a simple thing: it is to live from day to day, whatever the day brings, in this extraordinary unity, in this reconciliation with all people and all things, in this knowledge that death has no more power, in this truth of the resurrection. It does not really matter exactly what a Christian does from day to day. What matters is that whatever one does is done in honor of one's own life, given to one by God and restored to one in Christ, and in honor of the life into which all humans and all things are called. The only thing that really matters to live in Christ instead of death." **(William Stringfellow)**

"Baptism is like the wedding ring of salvation. I put on my wedding ring at the moment I decided to publicly declare my commitment to my wife. Putting on the ring did not make me married. I am no more married when I wear my ring than when I don't. But the demonstration of my commitment to my wife that the ring represents was a crucial first step in marriage. Had I refused to do it, my wife would have had reason to question my intentions. In the same way, baptism is an outward symbol of an inward covenant we've made in response to Jesus' offer of salvation." **(J.D. Greer)**

"Believing and being baptized are the two footsteps of one complete step: believing is one foot, and being baptized is the other, and these make one complete step." **(Witness Lee)**

"The Spaniards in Mexico and Peru used to baptize Indian infants and then immediately dash their brains out: by this means they secured these infants went to Heaven." **(Bertrand Russell)**

"Five types of baptism are mentioned in the New Testament, though only two of the five have to do with water. No wonder people become confused." **(Larry E. Dyer)**

Source: http://www.notable-quotes.com/b/baptism_quotes.html

Who Should Perform Baptisms

Once it is accepted that believers in Jesus Christ should be baptized to demonstrate that they accepted to walk anew with Christ, an obvious question is, who should perform baptisms? In many jurisdictions, a licence is required to perform certain ceremonies—marriage, funeral, baptism, etc. In the case of baptism, followers of Christ have a Great Commission to:

"Go therefore and make disciples of all nations, baptizing them in the name of the Father and of the Son and of the Holy Spirit, and teaching them to obey everything that I have commanded you." (Matthew 28:19-20).

It seems reasonable to think that the person performing baptism should be a disciple (follower) of Christ and a believer in the Christian doctrine. He or she should be a doer and not merely a sayer of the Word. It would indeed be odd to have a known criminal who had not renounced his or her sinful ways performing baptisms. Although the person's life may not be perfect, it should be substantially in accordance with God's will as revealed in Scripture.

Though not necessarily the case, baptism is usually performed by a denominational leader. This is especially the case when it is used as a means of membership into that church. There are cases where existing members baptize new members. There is nothing biblical against this practice, provided that a solemn occasion does not degenerate into triviality.

The performance of baptism should be regarded as a sacred duty and should not be treated lightly. It may not save you, but it proclaims that you are saved.

Baptism and Hope

We end this chapter by pointing out the relationship between baptism and hope. To begin with, if people do not have any hope, they are unlikely to submit to baptism. Baptism says that there is hope of a new life in the future with Christ. It symbolizes purification, rebirth, and the initiation into a community of faith. It holds a profound connection to the concept of hope, serving as a tangible expression of one's belief in a higher power and the promise of a brighter future.

Through baptism, individuals embark on a spiritual journey, leaving behind their old selves and embracing a new life imbued with hope. It represents a fresh start, a chance to be cleansed of past wrongdoings and embrace the limitless possibilities that lie ahead. Baptism instills a sense of hope by affirming the belief in divine grace, forgiveness, and the presence of a loving and guiding force in one's life. It serves as a reminder that no matter the trials and tribulations one may face, there is always hope for redemption, transformation, and spiritual growth. The act of baptism not only strengthens the individual's faith but also nurtures a collective hope within the faith community, fostering a sense of unity, support, and shared aspirations for a better world. In this way, baptism and hope are intertwined, as the ritual embodies the belief that through faith, one can find solace, purpose, and the unwavering assurance that there is always light even in the darkest of times.

Prayer

Our God and our Father, we thank you for enabling us to have a clearer understanding of the meaning and purpose of baptism. It is clear that You endorse the practice of baptism. We pray, Father, that You will help us to submit to baptism as an outward expression of our determination to adopt a life that is consistent with the life of Christ.

Amen

CHAPTER 13: THE TRINITY

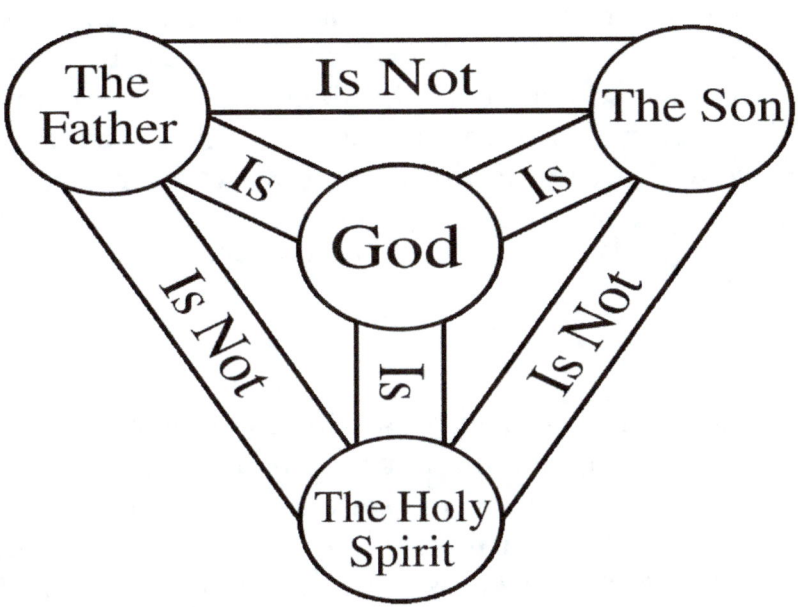

There is one God in three separate entities.

And Jesus came and said to them, "All authority in heaven and on earth has been given to me. Go therefore and make disciples of all nations, baptizing them in the name of the Father and of the Son and of the Holy Spirit, teaching them to observe all that I have commanded you. And behold, I am with you always, to the end of the age." (Matthew 28:18-20).

In Chapter 12, we discussed baptism as an outward manifestation of a decision to give up a sinful life and to live a life in total obedience to God's laws. It is worth noting that in most cases, the candidate is baptized in the name of the Father, Son, and Holy Spirit. In this chapter, we discuss those three persons in whose name people are baptized. They are (1) God, the Father, (2) God, the Son, and (3) God, the Holy Spirit. The idea of three persons in Father, Son, and Holy Spirit is easy enough to grasp, but the concept of three persons but one God, the Holy Trinity, is challenging, to say the least. The Trinity, also called the Godhead, are three beings working together in unity because they have a common objective and a common purpose. We will rely heavily on the Holy Scriptures to guide our discussion. We begin with the Holy Trinity/Godhead.

The Trinity/Godhead

The infinite concept of a triune God is difficult, if not impossible, to comprehend with our finite minds, but that does not negate its existence. There is but one God, creator of the universe, to whom we owe our existence and who deserves our praise and worship. He is omnipotent, omnipresent, and omniscient. It was He who said, "Let us make man in our own image..."; it is He who "so loved the world that He gave His only begotten Son, that whosoever believeth him should not perish but have everlasting life, and it is to Him we refer in the benediction, "the grace of the Lord Jesus Christ, and the love of God, and the communion of the Holy Spirit, be with you."

The Trinity in the Bible

The concept of a triune God appears in the Bible on several occasions. Perhaps the most evident was at the baptism of Jesus by John the Baptist. The Bible records it thus:

Then Jesus came from Galilee to the Jordan to be baptized by John But John tried to deter him, saying, "I need to be baptized by you, and do you come to me?" Jesus replied, "Let it be so now; it is proper for us to do this to fulfill all righteousness." Then John consented. As soon as Jesus was baptized, he went up out of the water. At that moment heaven was opened, and he saw the Spirit of God descending like a dove and alighting on him. And a voice from heaven said, "This is my Son, whom I love; with him I am well pleased." (Matthew 3:13-17)

Jesus, the Son, was present to be baptized. The Holy Spirit was present in the form of a dove, witnessing the baptism, and God, the Father was there expressing pleasure at the step that the Son had taken.

Here are some other instances.

yet for us there is but one God, the Father, from whom all things came and for whom we live; and there is but one Lord, Jesus Christ, through whom all things came and through whom we live **(1 Corinthians 8:6)**

Now the Lord is the Spirit, and where the Spirit of the Lord is, there is freedom **(2 Corinthians 3:17)**

May the grace of the Lord Jesus Christ, and the love of God, and the fellowship of the Holy Spirit be with you all **(2 Corinthians 13:14)**

For in Christ all the fullness of the Deity lives in bodily form, **(Colossians 2:9)**

For to us a child is born, to us a son is given, and the government will be on his shoulders. And he will be called Wonderful Counselor, Mighty God, Everlasting Father, Prince of Peace **(Isaiah 9:6)**

The Word became flesh and made his dwelling among us. We have seen his glory, the glory of the one and only Son, who came from the Father, full of grace and truth. **(John 1:14)**

I and the Father are one. **(John 10:30)**

The angel answered, "The Holy Spirit will come on you, and the power of the Most High will overshadow you. So the holy one to be born will be called the Son of God. **(Luke 1:35)**

"The virgin will conceive and give birth to a son, and they will call him Immanuel" (which means "God with us"). **(Matthew 1:23)**

Therefore go and make disciples of all nations, baptizing them in the name of the Father and of the Son and of the Holy Spirit, **(Matthew 28:19)**

And I will ask the Father, and he will give you another advocate to help you and be with you forever— the Spirit of truth. The world cannot accept him, because it neither sees him nor knows him. But you know him, for he lives with you and will be in you. **(John 14:16-17)**

For the kingdom of God is not a matter of eating and drinking, but of righteousness, peace and joy in the Holy Spirit, because anyone who serves Christ in this way is pleasing to God and receives human approval. **(Romans 14:17-18)**

For there are three that testify: the Spirit, the water and the blood; and the three are in agreement. **(1 John 5:7-8)**

Peter, an apostle of Jesus Christ, To God's elect, exiles scattered throughout the provinces of Pontus, Galatia, Cappadocia, Asia and Bithynia, who have been chosen according to the foreknowledge of God the Father, through the sanctifying work of the Spirit, to be obedient to Jesus Christ and sprinkled with his blood: Grace and peace be yours in abundance. **(1 Peter 1:1-2)**

Now it is God who makes both us and you stand firm in Christ. He anointed us, set his seal of ownership on us, and put his Spirit in our hearts as a deposit, guaranteeing what is to come. **(2 Corinthians 1:21-22)**

There are different kinds of gifts, but the same Spirit distributes them. There are different kinds of service, but the same Lord. There are different kinds of working, but in all of them and in everyone it is the same God at work. **(1 Corinthians 12:4-6)**

There is one body and one Spirit, just as you were called to one hope when you were called; one Lord, one faith, one baptism; one God and Father of all, who is over all and through all and in all. **(Ephesians 4:4-6)**

The Son is the image of the invisible God, the firstborn over all creation. For in him all things were created: things in heaven and on earth, visible and invisible, whether thrones or powers or rulers or authorities; all things have been created through him and for him. He is before all things, and in him all things hold together. **(Colossians 1:15-17)**

Jesus answered: "Don't you know me, Philip, even after I have been among you such a long time? Anyone who has seen me has seen the Father. How can you say, 'Show us the Father'? Don't you believe that I am in the Father, and that the Father is in me? The words I say to you I do not speak on my own authority. Rather, it is the Father, living in me, who is doing his work. Believe me when I say that I am in the Father and the Father is in me; or at least believe on the evidence of the works themselves. **(John 14:9-11)**

In your relationships with one another, have the same mindset as Christ Jesus: Who, being in very nature God, did not consider equality with God something to be used to his own advantage; rather, he made himself nothing by taking the very nature of a servant, being made in human likeness. And being found in appearance as a man, he humbled himself by becoming obedient to death— even death on a cross! **(Philippians 2:5-8)**

I and the Father are one." Again his Jewish opponents picked up stones to stone him, but Jesus said to them, "I have shown you many good works from the Father. For which of these do you stone me?" "We are not stoning you for any good work," they replied, "but for blasphemy, because you, a mere man, claim to be God." Jesus answered them, "Is it not written in your Law, 'I have said you are "gods" '? If he called them 'gods,' to whom the word of God came—and Scripture cannot be set aside— what about the one whom the Father set apart as his very own and sent into the world? Why then do you accuse me of blasphemy because I said, 'I am God's Son'? **(John 10:30-36)**

God the Father

God the Father is the only supreme being. He is Almighty and ruler of all. He is the one to whom Jesus prayed when he said, "Our Father which art in heaven", and again when he prayed, "Father forgive them because they don't know what they are doing. God the Father is the Father of us all who loves us with an everlasting love. No earthly father could love us as much as God the Father loves us. It is He who sent his only Son Jesus to die in our stead. It is He who cares so much about us that he knows even the number of hairs on our heads. It is He who numbers our days. God the Father sustains us; He sends the sunshine and the rain, and the air we breathe. It is in His image that human beings were created and He knows everything from the beginning to the end.

God the Son

God the Son is the one we know as Jesus Christ our Lord and Saviour. He is the one who came to earth as a baby born of the Virgin Mary. He is the one who was accused of blasphemy because he claimed to be God. God the Son lived on earth like a man, born in Nazareth, preached to the multitude, led his disciples, healed the sick, and raised the dead. He was crucified, He was buried, and He was resurrected. It is He of whom it is written:

He left the splendor of heaven
Knowing His destiny
Was the lonely hill of Golgotha
There to lay down His life for me. **(Dottie Rambo)**

Pathways to a Brighter Future

It is He of whom the songwriter wrote:
I've found a Friend, oh, such a Friend!
He loved me ere I knew Him;
He drew me with the cords of love,
And thus He bound me to Him
And round my heart still closely twine
Those ties which naught can sever,
For I am His, and He is mine,
Forever and forever. **(James G. Small)**

It is by believing in Jesus Christ the Son that we can obtain salvation.

God the Holy Spirit

The third person of the Godhead is the Holy Spirit. Perhaps we underestimate the importance of the Holy Spirit in our lives. The Bible tells us that the Holy Spirit plays a vital role in our communication with God the Father.

Likewise the Spirit helps us in our weakness. For we do not know what to pray for as we ought, but the Spirit himself intercedes for us with groanings too deep for words. (Romans 8:26)

The Holy Spirit helps us to understand spiritual things. When we study the Holy Scriptures, the Holy Spirit enlightens us like a "lamp unto our feet and a light to our path." The Holy Spirit lives within us. As Paul expresses it,

What? know ye not that your body is the temple of the Holy Ghost which is in you, which ye have of God, and ye are not your own? For ye are bought with a price: therefore glorify God in your body, and in your spirit, which are God's. (1Corinthians 19-20)

The Holy Spirit fills us with love, peace, longsuffering, kindness, goodness, faithfulness, gentleness, and self-control, which Paul describes as the fruit of the Spirit (Galatians 5:22).

Hope and the Trinity

One of my best friends knew I was writing a book on hope, so she asked how it was coming along. I informed her that I was then writing on the Trinity. In surprise, she asked, "The Trinity in a book on Hope?" I reminded her that God the Father is the source of hope, that we have hope in the second coming of the Son, and that through the Holy Spirit, we endure tribulations and look with optimism for a better life in the future.

The benevolence, might, and omniscience of God the Father inspire hope in Christians. They know that an all-knowing, all-seeing God cares about them and will not fail to keep His promises. Through the birth, life, ministry on earth, death, and resurrection of God the Son, his followers have hope of eternal life in the home that He has gone to prepare for His believers. Finally, hope is experienced through the presence of the Holy Spirit. The Spirit's role is to guide, comfort, and empower believers, acting as a constant source of hope in their lives. The Holy Spirit brings spiritual gifts and enables individuals to persevere through trials, inspiring them to have hope in God's promises and the fulfillment of His plans.

In summary, hope and the Trinity are intimately intertwined in the Christian experience. The Father, Son, and Holy Spirit collectively embody hope, offering believers a steadfast assurance of a brighter future and a deeper connection with God. Through their divine unity, the Trinity instills hope, providing solace, strength, and a sense of purpose in the face of life's challenges.

Prayer

Most kind and ever-loving Father, our Creator and Redeemer, we thank you for your love, mercy, and grace. We pray for a more comprehensive understanding of the workings of the Holy Trinity in our lives.

Amen

HOPE

CHAPTER 14: ANGELS

Angels are God's holy messengers.

Are they not all ministering spirits sent out to serve for the sake of those who are to inherit salvation? (Hebrews 1:14)

Stories about angels abound. We often conceive of them as sweet, innocent, good-natured creatures. To many of us, they are associated with guarding and protecting us from harm and danger, and with delivering messages from superior beings. What exactly are angels? Where do they come from? What are their attributes? What is their role or function? Who are some famous angels? What does the Bible say about angels? These questions will be answered in this chapter.

What are Angels

Angels are created beings between the Godhead and human beings. They are spirits rather than mortal. The word "angel" means "messenger" or "assistant." Human beings are made a little lower than the angels. The psalmist declared:

For thou hast made him a little lower than the angels, and hast crowned him with glory and honour. (Psalm 8:5)

Bible Verses about Angels

A great deal of what many people know about angels comes from the Bible. These angelic beings are mentioned about 273 times in more than 51% of the books of the Bible. Here are some important Bible verses that will enlighten us about the celestial beings called angels.

In the same way, I tell you, there is rejoicing in the presence of the angels of God over one sinner who repents. **(Luke 15:10)**

Are not all angels ministering spirits sent to serve those who will inherit salvation? **(Hebrews 1:14)**

For he will command his angels concerning you to guard you in all your ways; **(Psalms 91:11)**

HOPE

At the resurrection people will neither marry nor be given in marriage; they will be like the angels in heaven. **(Matthew 22:30 (NIV)**

Then I saw another angel flying in midair, and he had the eternal gospel to proclaim to those who live on the earth—to every nation, tribe, language and people. **(Revelation 14:6)**

And the angels who did not keep their positions of authority but abandoned their proper dwelling—these he has kept in darkness, bound with everlasting chains for judgment on the great Day. **(Jude 1:6)**

For he will command his angels concerning you to guard you in all your ways. They will bear you up on their hands lest you strike your foot against a stone. **(Psalm 91:11-12)**

See that you do not despise one of these little ones. For I tell you that their angels in heaven always see the face of my Father in heaven." **(Matthew 18:10)**

And suddenly there was with the angel a multitude of the heavenly host praising God and saying, 'Glory to God in the highest, and on earth peace among those with whom he is pleased!' **(Luke 2:13-14)**

Now war arose in heaven, Michael and his angels fighting against the dragon. And the dragon and his angels fought back, but he was defeated, and there was no longer any place for them in heaven." **(Revelation 12:7-9)**

Let brotherly love continue. Do not neglect to show hospitality to strangers, for thereby some have entertained angels unawares. **(Hebrews 13:1-2)**

Pathways to a Brighter Future

> The angel of the Lord encamps around those who fear him, and delivers them. **(Psalm 34:7)**

> But during the night an angel of the Lord opened the prison doors and brought them out, and said, **(Acts 5:19)**

> Suddenly an angel of the Lord appeared, and a light shone in the cell. He struck Peter on the side and woke him up. 'Quick, get up!' he said, and the chains fell off Peter's wrists. **(Acts 12:7)**

> But when he had considered this, behold, an angel of the Lord appeared to him in a dream, saying, "Joseph, son of David, do not be afraid to take Mary as your wife; for the Child who has been conceived in her is of the Holy Spirit. **(Matthew 1:20)**

> Then the devil left Him; and behold, angels came and began to minister to Him. **(Matthew 4:11)**

> Then the angel of the Lord went out and struck 185,000 in the camp of the Assyrians; and when men arose early in the morning, behold, all of these were dead. **(Isaiah 37:36)**

> And there appeared to him an angel from heaven, strengthening him. **(Luke 22:43)**

From these passages of scripture we learn, among other things, that angels watch over us, protect us, and guide us; that they are ministering spirits; that they are our guardians; that they have eyes and sometimes appear as men; that they strengthen those who trust in God.

Types or Categories of Angels

The Bible records three types of angels:

Cherubim

Seraphim

Living Creatures

Let us look quickly at each type.

Cherubim

Cherubim is the plural form of cherub. In Genesis 3:24, cherubim are recorded as guarding the entrance to the Garden of Eden after Adam and Eve were evicted from their Edenic home.

After he drove the man out, he placed on the east side[a] of the Garden of Eden cherubim and a flaming sword flashing back and forth to guard the way to the tree of life.

The Bible also records in Psalm 18:10, that God rides upon the cherubim.

And He rode upon a cherub and flew; yea, He flew upon the wings of the wind.

In Ezekiel 10:1-19 we learn that the cherubim support the throne of God.

When the cherubim departed, they lifted their wings and rose up from the ground in my sight with the wheels beside them; and they stood still at the entrance

Pathways to a Brighter Future

of the east gate of the LORD'S house, and the glory of the God of Israel hovered over them.

Saraphim

Seraphim is the plural form of seraph. They are mentioned only once in the Bible in Isaiah 6:2-3. There we read:

Above him were seraphim, each with six wings: With two wings they covered their faces, with two they covered their feet, and with two they were flying. And they were calling to one another:

*"Holy, holy, holy is the L*ORD *Almighty; the whole earth is full of his glory."*

From this passage, we gather that seraphim have six wings, that they fly, that they cover their faces, and that they surround the throne of God.

Living Creatures

Living creatures are another type of celestial beings. The Bible speaks of these creatures. For example, in Revelation 4:8, they are recorded as worshipping God continually.

Each of the four living creatures had six wings and was covered with eyes all around, even under its wings. Day and night they never stop saying:

"'Holy, holy, holy is the Lord God Almighty, who was, and is, and is to come."

Names of Angels

The Bible records that there are countless thousands of angels. Witness the following passages:

No, you have come to Mount Zion, to the city of the living God, the heavenly Jerusalem, and to countless thousands of angels in a joyful gathering. **(Hebrews 12:22)**

"You have made them to be a kingdom and priests to our God; and they will reign upon the earth." Then I looked, and I heard the voice of many angels around the throne and the living creatures and the elders; and the number of them was myriads of myriads, and thousands of thousands, saying with a loud voice, "Worthy is the Lamb that was slain to receive power and riches and wisdom and might and honor and glory and blessing." **(Revelation. 5:10-12**

However, of the myriads of myriads of angels, only four are given particular names in the Bible. They are:

1. Gabriel

2. Michael

3. Lucifer

4. Abaddon (Apollyon)

We will discuss each one in turn, beginning with Gabriel.

Gabriel

Most Christians are well aware of the angel Gabriel. He appeared to Daniel, and to the priest

Zechariah, and finally to Mary. The occasions are as recorded below:

While I, Daniel, was watching the vision and trying to understand it, there before me stood one who looked like a man. And I heard a man's voice from the Ulai calling, "Gabriel, tell this man the meaning of the vision" (Daniel 8:15-16).

While I was still in prayer, Gabriel, the man I had seen in the earlier vision, came to me in swift flight about the time of the evening sacrifice. He instructed me and said to me, "Daniel, I have now come to give you insight and understanding" (Daniel 9:21-22).

Then an angel of the Lord appeared to him... When Zechariah saw him, he was startled and gripped with fear. But the angel said to him: "Do not be afraid, Zechariah; your prayer has been heard. Your wife Elizabeth will bear you a son, and you are to call him John."

Zechariah asked the angel, "How can I be sure of this? I am an old man and my wife is well along in years."

The angel said to him, "I am Gabriel. I stand in the presence of God, and I have been sent to speak to you and to tell you this good news. And now you will be silent and not able to speak until the day this happens, because you did not believe my words, which will come true at their appointed time" (Luke 1:11-13,18-20).

In the sixth month of Elizabeth's pregnancy, God sent the angel Gabriel to Nazareth, a town in Galilee, to a virgin pledged to be married to a man named Joseph, a descendant of David. The virgin's name was Mary. The angel went to her and said, "Greetings, you who are highly favored! The Lord is with you." Mary was greatly troubled at his words and wondered what kind of greeting this might be (Luke 1:26-29).

It seems as if the angel Gabriel can assume the form of a man; he has the ability to fly; he has the ability to speak; and he is aware of what is going on on earth.

Michael

Michael is a well-known angel from Scripture. Seemingly, he is an angel of rank and not just any ordinary angel. Here are some Scriptual references to the angel Michael.

"Michael, one of the chief princes, came to help me, because I was detained there with the king of Persia" (Daniel 10:13).

But even the archangel Michael, when he was disputing with the devil about the body of Moses, did not himself dare to condemn him for slander but said, "The Lord rebuke you!" (Jude 1:9)

Then war broke out in heaven. Michael and his angels fought against the dragon, and the dragon and his angels fought back (Revelation 12:7).

"At that time Michael, the great prince who protects your people, will arise" (Daniel 12:1).

We learn that Michael is one of the chief princes, that he is an archangel, that he is a leader of angels, and that he is a prince and protector, and that he fought against the Devil.

Lucifer

You will recall that Lucifer was the name of Satan before he rebelled against God's government and was cast out of heaven. This is what Scripture says of Lucifer:

This is what the Sovereign Lord says: "You were the seal of perfection, full of wisdom and perfect in beauty. You were in Eden, the garden of God; ...Your settings and mountings were made of gold; on the day you were created they were prepared. You were anointed as a guardian cherub, for so I ordained you. You were on the holy mount of God... You were blameless in your ways from the day you were created till wickedness was found in you Your heart became proud on account of your beauty, and you corrupted your wisdom because of your splendor. So I threw you to the earth (Ezekiel 28:12-19).

To know more about this fallen angel and his final doom, look at Chapter 11.

Abaddon or Apollyon

The last named angel in the Bible is Abaddon or Apollyon which means Destroyer. Here is the Biblical reference to that angel:

And the fifth angel blew his trumpet, and I saw a star fallen from heaven to earth, and he was given the key to the shaft of the bottomless pit. Then from the smoke came locusts on the earth, and they were given power like the power of scorpions of the earth. They had as king over them the angel of the Abyss, whose name in Hebrew is Abaddon and in Greek is Apollyon that is, Destroyer (Revelation 9:1-3,11).

The Nature of Angels

On the basis of the Bible, we gather some information about the characteristics of angels. We identify them in this section.

Angels are Immortal

Unlike human beings, angels are spirits who are not subject to the physical limitations of human beings. Unlike human beings, angels can be invisible. In Hebrews 1:14 we read:

Are not all angels ministering spirits sent to serve those who will inherit salvation?

We know also that they do not die like human beings do.

and they can no longer die; for they are like the angels. They are God's children, since they are children of the resurrection **(Luke 20:36)**

Although they are spirits, angels have the ability to relate to the physical realm. We see evidence of this from the following passage:

There was a violent earthquake, for an angel of the Lord came down from heaven and, going to the tomb, rolled back the stone and sat on it **(Matthew 28:2)**

Angels have Superhuman Power

The following passages of Scripture easily lead to the conclusion that angels have superhuman power:

But during the night an angel of the Lord opened the doors of the jail and brought them out (Acts 5:19)

Pathways to a Brighter Future

So Peter was kept in prison, but the church was earnestly praying to God for him. The night before Herod was to bring him to trial, Peter was sleeping between two soldiers, bound with two chains, and sentries stood guard at the entrance. Suddenly an angel of the Lord appeared and a light shone in the cell. He struck Peter on the side and woke him up. "Quick, get up!" he said, and the chains fell off Peter's wrists. Then the angel said to him, "Put on your clothes and sandals." And Peter did so. "Wrap your cloak around you and follow me," the angel told him. Peter followed him out of the prison, but he had no idea that what the angel was doing was really happening; he thought he was seeing a vision. They passed the first and second guards and came to the iron gate leading to the city. It opened for them by itself, and they went through it. When they had walked the length of one street, suddenly the angel left him. Then Peter came to himself and said, "Now I know without a doubt that the Lord has sent his angel and rescued me from Herod's clutches and from everything the Jewish people were hoping would happen." (Acts 12:5-11)

But the men (angels) inside reached out and pulled Lot back into the house and shut the door. Then they struck the men who were at the door of the house, young and old, with blindness so that they could not find the door (Genesis 19:10-11)

Angels are Divine Beings

We make this claim based on Scripture. Witness the following passages:

"In the visions I saw while lying in bed, I looked, and there before me was a holy one, a messenger, coming down from heaven. "'The decision is announced by messengers, the holy ones declare the verdict, so that the living may know that the Most High is sovereign over all

kingdoms on earth and gives them to anyone he wishes and sets over them the lowliest of people.' (Daniel 4:13, 17)

And Enoch also, the seventh from Adam, prophesied of these, saying, Behold, the Lord cometh with ten thousands of his saints, (Jude 14)

they, too, will drink the wine of God's fury, which has been poured full strength into the cup of his wrath. They will be tormented with burning sulfur in the presence of the holy angels and of the Lamb. (Revelation 14:10)

Quotes about Angels

The following quotes about angels will help to stimulate your ideas about these mysterious beings and reveal some thoughts and perceptions about them. Some are humorous, some are serious, while others may be inspiring.

All that I am, or hope to be, I owe to my angel mother. **(Abraham Lincoln)**

Black as the devil, hot as hell, pure as an angel, sweet as love. **(Charles Maurice de Talleyrand)**

I am good, but not an angel. I do sin, but I am not the devil. I am just a small girl in a big world trying to find someone to love. **(Marilyn Monroe)**

No, I never saw an angel, but it is irrelevant whether I saw one or not. I feel their presence around me. **(Paulo Coelho)**

I'm no angel, but I'm no monster, either. **(R. Kelly)**

It is impossible to see the angel unless you first have a notion of it. **(James Hillman)**

The way people come into your life when you need them, it's wonderful and it happens in so many ways. It's like having an angel. Somebody comes along and helps you get right. **(Stevie Ray Vaughan)**

The peasant must always be helped technically, economically, morally and culturally. The guerrilla fighter will be a sort of guiding angel who has fallen into the zone, helping the poor always and bothering the rich as little as possible in the first phases of the war. **(Che Guevara)**

Don't put wings on me; I am no angel. **(Diego Costa)**

I am an angel. I was sent here from God to heal. **(Kevin Hart)**

I do not want to be the angel of any home: I want for myself what I want for other women, absolute equality. After that is secured, then men and women can take turns being angels. **(Agnes Macphail)**

Grace, like an angel of mercy, makes his voice heard sweet and clear, repeating the story of the cross, the matchless love of Jesus. **(Ellen G. White)**

Kind words are the music of the world. They have a power which seems to be beyond natural causes, as if they were some angel's song, which had lost its way and come on Earth, and sang on undyingly, smiting the hearts of men with sweetest wounds, and putting for the while an angel's nature into us. **(Frederick William Faber)**

In the Christian world... it is believed that angels were created at the beginning, and that heaven was formed of them; and that the Devil or Satan was an angel of light, who, becoming rebellions, was cast down with his crew, and that this was the origin of hell. **(Emanuel Swedenborg)**

The day I got my first letter from a fan, I felt like I'd been touched by an angel. **(Selena Gomez)**

When I look back on my life, I wonder how I survived - my mother said I had a guardian angel. **(Micky Dolenz)**

Source: https://www.brainyquote.com/topics/angel-quotes

Hope and Angels

We have learnt that angels are spiritual beings with superhuman power, and that they are messengers carrying out the will of God. It is comforting to know that we are not alone; there are angels ready to help us. Hope is a powerful force that resides within the human spirit, capable of igniting a spark of optimism even in the darkest of times. Hope reminds us that there is always a glimmer of light at the end of the tunnel, and that better days lie ahead.

Angels are often depicted as ethereal beings of light, symbolizing purity, protection, and divine guidance. They embody the essence of hope, serving as messengers of comfort and solace in times of distress. Angels are believed to watch over us, providing reassurance and inspiring us to keep faith alive. They offer a reminder that we are not alone in our struggles, and that there is a greater purpose guiding our journey. Their presence evokes a sense of peace and an unwavering belief that goodness prevails, instilling hope in our hearts when we need it most.

Together, hope and angels combine to remind us of the resilience of the human spirit and the boundless possibilities that lie ahead. They encourage us to hold on to our dreams, to persevere through challenges, and to embrace the power of belief. In the presence of angels, hope shines brightly, and we are reminded that even in the face of adversity, miracles can happen, and our spirits can soar.

Poem

The Angel

I dreamt a dream! What can it mean?
And that I was a maiden Queen
Guarded by an Angel mild:
Witless woe was ne'er beguiled!

And I wept both night and day,
And he wiped my tears away;
And I wept both day and night,
And hid from him my heart's delight.

So, he took his wings, and fled;
Then the morn blushed rosy red.
I dried my tears, and armed my fears
With ten-thousand shields and spears.

Soon my Angel came again;
I was armed, he came in vain;
For the time of youth was fled,
And grey hairs were on my head. **William Blake**

Prayer

Almighty God, creator of heaven and earth, help us to understand more about Your Holy angels and their roles in our sphere. Father, our world is fraught with danger, pitfalls, and snares. We pray that You will send Your Holy angels to protect us as we go to and fro, and to watch over us as we sleep. We thank you in Jesus' name.

Amen

Pathways to a Brighter Future

CHAPTER 15: THE STATE OF THE DEAD

After we die, we lie in our graves lifeless and knowing nothing.

For the living know they will die; but the dead do not know anything, nor have they any longer a reward, for their memory is forgotten (Ecclesiastes 9:5).

When I was a boy, about 12 years old, my younger brother and I were walking home from our farm at dusk. A very good-natured lady (let's call her Miss Ellie) had recently died. On the lonely road, less than ten minutes away from our home, Miss Ellie passed us going in the opposite direction. Forgetting that Miss Ellie was dead, we greeted her with the usual, "Good evening, Miss Ellie." To my surprise, the usually good-natured lady

HOPE

did not respond. Immediately I remembered that she was dead. I looked back only to see what appeared to be Miss Ellie entering a cane field and disappearing from view. Thereupon, I asked my brother if he saw Miss Ellie entering the cane field, to which he replied in the affirmative.

As soon as I arrived at home, I related the incident to my parents. My father's explanation was that it was not Miss Ellie whom we saw. It was the devil or one of his angels imitating her. He stressed that people who are dead cannot walk or task. I believed him because he was a preacher, but more so because he was my Dad. I received my first lesson on the state of the dead.

Where Are the Dead?

We will rely solely on the Holy Scriptures to answer this very controversial question. In obituaries, at funerals, and elsewhere, we often hear statements to the effect that people who have died have gone to heaven. Many people who hold that view claim to believe in the resurrection when Christ will wake up the righteous dead from their graves and take them to heaven. Obviously, these views are contradictory. If the righteous dead are already in heaven with the Lord, then the idea of a resurrection is useless. There will be no one to resurrect because they will be in heaven.

The Bible has not left us in darkness concerning the state of the dead. According to God's Word, when people die, they no longer exist. When we are alive, we know things, we entertain thoughts, we have plans, and we see, feel, hear, taste, and smell. None of these things pertains to the dead. The Bible tells us:

For the living know that they shall die: but the dead know not any thing... (Ecclesiastes 9:5).

But a man dies and is laid low; man breathes his last, and where is he? As waters fail from a lake and a river wastes away and dries up, so a man lies down and rises not again; till the heavens are no more he will not awake or be roused out of his sleep. (Job 14:10-12)

So, where are the dead? They are in their graves, at the bottom of oceans, or wherever their bodies were placed when they died. They cannot use any of their senses or move about because they are lifeless.

Body, Spirit, and Soul

Much of the misunderstanding surrounding the state of the dead arises from confusion about the body, spirit, and soul. Let us explore Biblical truths about the relationship between the body, spirit, and soul.

The Body

God created the body with His own hands out of the dust of the earth. This includes all the parts of the physical body such as the limbs and organs.

The Spirit

The spirit is the breath of life. Without it, the body is dead. It is the spirit that gives life to the body. The spirit by itself cannot see, think, speak, or hear.

The Soul

The soul is a composite of the body and the spirit. It is a living being. It does not exist apart from the body and the spirit.

The Relationship between Body, Spirit, and Soul

The relationship between body, spirit, and soul can be illustrated by the following equation:

BODY + SPIRIT = SOUL

↓ ↓ ↓

Dust of the ground + Breath of life = Living soul

The Bible says: And the Lord God formed man of the dust of the ground, and breathed into his nostrils the breath of life; and man became a living soul. **(Genesis 2:7).**

Now, what happens when we die should make more sense. The Bible states clearly:

Then shall the dust return to the earth as it was: and the spirit shall return unto God who gave it. **(Ecclesiastes 12:7)**

The body returns to the earth from which it was taken, and the breath of life returns to God who gave it in the first place.

The Death of the Soul

There are many who claim that the soul never dies. Now that we have a clearer understanding of the soul, we know that such a doctrine is false. We have seen that the soul is a composite of body and breath. It is therefore illogical to claim that the body dies but not the soul. The Bible leaves no doubt at all about the death of the soul. It says:

The soul that sinneth, it shall die. The son shall not bear the iniquity of the father, neither shall the father bear the iniquity of the son: the righteousness of the righteous shall be upon him, and the wickedness of the wicked shall be upon him. **(Ezekiel 18:20)**

Note also that there can be no substitution.

When Eve (and Adam) disobeyed God and ate the forbidden fruit, they did not die from fruit poisoning. They died because they sinned. The living being (i.e., the soul) died. Is the soul immortal? The answer is emphatically no. The soul is mortal. It dies because of sin.

Spirit and Body Re-united

At death, the spirit (breath) leaves the body. The body (dust) returns to the earth from whence it came, and the breath (spirit) returns to God. Is this the end of the story? Not at all. The Bible assures us that there will be a resurrection of the dead when the body and the spirit will be reunited. Here are some passages from the Holy Scriptures to support this claim:

Many of those who sleep in the dust of the ground will awake, these to everlasting life, but the others to disgrace and everlasting contempt. **(Daniel 12:2)**

Do not marvel at this; for an hour is coming, in which all who are in the tombs will hear His voice, and will come forth; those who did the good deeds to a resurrection of life, those who committed the evil deeds to a resurrection of judgment. (John 5:28-29)

And I saw the dead, the great and the small, standing before the throne, and books were opened; and another book was opened, which is the book of life; and the dead were judged from the things which were written in the books, according to their deeds. And the sea gave up the dead which were in it, and death and Hades gave up the dead which were in them; and they were judged, every one of them according to their deeds. (Revelation 20:12, 13)

...in a moment, in the twinkling of an eye, at the last trumpet; for the trumpet will sound, and the dead will be raised imperishable, and we will be changed.
(1 Corinthians 15:52)

For the Lord Himself will descend from heaven with a shout, with the voice of the archangel and with the trumpet of God, and the dead in Christ will rise first.
(1 Thessalonians 4:16)

Then I saw thrones, and people sat upon them—those to whom authority to judge was given. And I saw the souls of those who had been beheaded because of their testimony for Yeshua and because of the word of God. They had not worshiped the beast or his image, nor had they received his mark on their forehead or on their hand. And they came to life and reigned with the Messiah for a thousand years. **(Revelation 20:4, 5)**

The Bible teaches that the soul that sins shall surely die. However, through the sacrificial death of Jesus on the cross, and through our belief in the Lord Jesus Christ, our bodies and spirits will be reunited. We will live again.

Hope and the Resurrection

Christians ought not to be afraid of death because they know what it is. It is not a state of torment or anguish or terror. It is not the end. The Apostle Paul advises us not to be ignorant about those who die. Hope makes us different. Because of hope, we need not be despondent when our loved ones die. We have hope, a feeling of expectation and desire, that the time will come when body and spirit will be reunited, and the dead shall rise. Just as Jesus died and arose from the dead, so too will we. We can comfort one another with this hope:

For the Lord himself shall descend from heaven with a shout, with the voice of the archangel, and with the trump of God: and the dead in Christ shall rise first: Then we which are alive and remain shall be caught up together with them in the clouds, to meet the Lord in the air: and so shall we ever be with the Lord.
(1Thessalonians 4:16, 17)

Christians live in the hope of the resurrection that brings life and begins our being with the Lord forever.

Prayer

Father in Heaven, there is a great deal of confusion about the state of the dead. We are happy that you have not left us ignorant on this important issue. We thank You that Your word, the Holy Bible, can lead us into the truth about those who have passed on. Loving Father, in the event that we are still in the dark regarding the state of the dead, we pray that You will give us wisdom that will lead us out of darkness into Your marvelous light.

Amen

HOPE

CHAPTER 16: CRIME

Crimes have costs and benefits

Finally, brothers and sisters, whatever is true, whatever is noble, whatever is right, whatever is pure, whatever is lovely, whatever is admirable—if anything is excellent or praiseworthy—think about such things. (Philippians 4:8)

What is Crime?

Crime is not a new phenomenon. Most people have the idea that crime has something to do with wrongdoing, but they seem to know that not every wrongdoing is a crime. To provide a framework for our discussion, and to avoid confusion, we will provide a simple working definition of crime.

The Oxford English Dictionary defines crime simply as:

'An action or omission which constitutes an offence and is punishable by law'.

Note that one can commit a crime by doing something or by neglecting to do something. For example, in most jurisdictions, it is a crime to take someone else's property without his or her permission. It is called stealing. Similarly, failure of parents to provide food for their children is a crime in most civilized societies.

Types of Crimes

There are many different types of crimes, but they can be classified under the following four main categories:

- Crimes against a Person
- Crimes against Property
- Statutory crimes
- Financial crimes

Let us take a cursory look at each category.

Crimes against a Person

These crimes result in physical, mental or emotional harm to persons. Examples of crimes against persons include murder, kidnapping, torture, assault, battery, child abuse, and rape.

Crimes against Property

Crimes against property are varied and include depriving someone of the use of his or her property. Theft is a good example of a crime against property. Other common crimes against property include arson, trespassing, shoplifting, robbery, vandalism, and willful damage to property.

Statutory Crimes

Statutory crimes include those activities that are prohibited by statute. Like other prohibitive laws, the objective is to discourage individuals from engaging in certain activities. Statutory crimes include drug crimes, traffic offenses, and alcohol-related crimes.

Financial Crimes

Finally, financial crimes are those crimes that involve misrepresentation and fraud for financial gain. They are often equated with what is referred to as white color crime. Common examples of financial crimes are embezzlement, securities fraud, tax evasion, identity theft, blackmail, money laundering, and corporate fraud.

Sayings about Crimes

Reading what others have to say about crime gives you the opportunity to see and understand different aspects of crime as it is seen through different lenses. Some are humorous, some are wise, while others are thought-provoking and serious.

"By each crime and every kindness, we birth our future." **David Mitchell**

"Crime generally punishes itself." **Oliver Goldsmith**

"The infectiousness of crime is like that of the plague." **Napoleon Bonaparte**

"He reminds me of the man who murdered both his parents, and then when the sentence was about to be pronounced, pleaded for mercy on the grounds that he was orphan." **Abraham Lincoln**

"It's about time law enforcement got as organized as organized crime." **Rudy Giuliani**

"Organized crime in America takes in over forty billion dollars a year and spends very little on office supplies." **Woody Allen**

We don't seem to be able to check crime, so why not legalize it and then tax it out of business? **Will Rogers**

"Let the punishment fit the crime." **William Schwenck Gilbert**

"Crime does not pay as well as politics." **Alfred Newman**

"Punishment is not for revenge, but to lessen crime and reform the criminal." **Elizabeth Fry**

Poverty is the parent of revolution and crime. **Aristotle**

"It is shocking how many crimes the Bible contains. The Governor's wife should cut them all out and paste them into her scrapbook." **Margaret Atwood**

"Little crimes breed big crimes. You smile at little crimes and then big crimes blow your head off."
Terry Pratchett

"Rape is a more heinous crime than murder since the rape victim dies throughout the period she lives."
Amit Abraham

"In these electric times the criminal receives a cosmopolitan reputation. It is a privilege he shares with few other artists." **Israel Zangwill**

"For the powerful, crimes are those that others commit." **Noam Chomsky**

"To have once been a criminal is no disgrace. To remain a criminal is the disgrace." **Malcolm X**

"There are crimes of passion and crimes of logic. The boundary between them is not clearly defined."
Albert Camus

"Providence sees to it that no man gets happiness out of crime."
Conte Vittorio Alfieri

Source: https://www.coolnsmart.com/crime_quotes/

The Bible on Crime

Crime is of concern to most people. The Bible speaks out against wrongdoing. Since the Bible is such an influential book that is a guide for good living, it would be interesting to see what it has to say about crime. Here are some verses:

Pathways to a Brighter Future

For out of the heart proceed evil thoughts, murders, adulteries, fornications, thefts, false witness, blasphemies. **(Matthew 15:19)**

Let him who stole steal no longer, but rather let him labor, working with his hands what is good, that he may have something to give him who has need. **(Ephesians 4:28)**

You shall not murder. **(Exodus 20:13)**

You shall not steal. **(Exodus 20:15)**

You shall not give false testimony against your neighbor. **(Exodus 20:16)**

Hear the word of the LORD, You children of Israel, For the LORD brings a charge against the inhabitants of the land: There is no truth or mercy Or knowledge of God in the land. By swearing and lying, Killing and stealing and committing adultery, They break all restraint, With bloodshed upon bloodshed. Therefore the land will mourn; And everyone who dwells there will waste away With the beasts of the field And the birds of the air; Even the fish of the sea will be taken away. **(Hosea 4:1-3)**

He who strikes a man so that he dies shall surely be put to death. However, if he did not lie in wait, but God delivered him into his hand, then I will appoint for you a place where he may flee. "But if a man acts with premeditation against his neighbor, to kill him by treachery, you shall take him from My altar, that he may die. **(Exodus 21:12-14)**

Nor thieves, nor covetous, nor drunkards, nor revilers, nor extortioners will inherit the kingdom of God. **(1 Corinthians 6:10)**

Repay no one evil for evil. Have regard for good things in the sight of all men. If it is possible, as much as depends on you, live peaceably with all men. Beloved, do not avenge yourselves, but rather give place to wrath; for it is written, "Vengeance is Mine, I will repay," says the Lord. **(Romans 12:17-19)**

Let every soul be subject to the governing authorities. For there is no authority except from God, and the authorities that exist are appointed by God. Therefore whoever resists the authority resists the ordinance of God, and those who resist will bring judgment on themselves. For rulers are not a terror to good works, but to evil. Do you want to be unafraid of the authority? Do what is good, and you will have praise from the same. For he is God's minister to you for good. But if you do evil, be afraid; for he does not bear the sword in vain; for he is God's minister, an avenger to execute wrath on him who practices evil. **(Romans 13:1-4)**

Clearly, the Bible does not condone crime; on the contrary, it admonishes us to eschew it.

The Benefits and Costs of Crime

The Benefits of Crime

It seems incongruous to talk about the benefits of crime, but if rational people willfully commit crimes, then it must be because they believe they reap some kind of benefits from their criminal activities. We need not spend an inordinate amount of time discussing the advantages of crime, but we think it is worth pointing out that crime has benefits. Some of the benefits of crime for the criminals are the following:

- **Choice of working hours** To some extent, criminals can choose their hours of work

- **Recognition** Criminals may gain recognition among their peers and even among members of the society. They may be known though not for their good deeds.

- **Ill-gotten gains** Many criminals enrich themselves through theft, robbery, forgery, drug trafficking, human trafficking, and other such crimes.

- **Satisfaction from revenge** Some crimes result from people seeking revenge for what they perceive as wrongdoing against them—a kind of retributive justice. For example, setting fire to a building owned by someone who sexually abused your child.

- **Adrenaline rush** Criminals may actually enjoy criminal activities as they provide a physical feeling of intense excitement and stimulation caused by the release of adrenaline in the same way that race car drivers and divers feel a rapid hormonal release in the body.

Note that the benefits of crime accrue to the individual, not to the society.

The Costs of Crime

The costs of crime far outweigh the benefits. They can be analyzed in terms of cost to the criminal, cost to the victims, and cost to society.

Costs to the Criminals

Some of the costs to criminals include:

- **Tools and equipment** Some crimes may require certain tools and specialized equipment. A robbery might require guns, electric drills, and screwdrivers.

- **Time** Particular crimes may involve cost in terms of planning time, time to case the scene of the crime, and time to execute the crime.

- **Legal fees** People who commit crimes often need lawyers to defend them in a court of law. If they have reputations as criminals, it may be quite expensive to get lawyers to plea their cases.

- **Payroll** Depending on the nature and scale of the crime, criminals may employ others to carry out certain functions such as driving. They may even have law enforcement officers on their staff to facilitate their illegal activities.

- **Punishment** If caught, the criminal may suffer penalties ranging from a small fine to imprisonment or even death.

- **Remorse** The criminal may experience feelings of remorse which make it difficult for him or her to sleep. This may result in serious physical and emotional problems.

- **Ostracism** It often happens that the criminal is ostracized from the community. He or she is not welcome at certain events, and his or her company is shunned.

Costs to the Victims

The victims of crime bear unwanted costs, some of which are the following:

- **Bodily injuries** Sadly, many crimes, especially violent crimes, end up causing bodily injuries to the victims. They may end up in hospitals costing a great deal of money.

- **Loss of income** The victims of crime may suffer from significant loss of income because of their inability to work. Thus, their families may also incur the cost of crime.

- **Loss of property** Crimes such theft and arson may result in the loss of or damage to the property of the victim. This may include property of sentimental or historical value that cannot be replaced.

- **Extreme fear** The victims of crime may suffer from extreme fear and other psychological and emotional problems.

- **Loss of life** The ultimate cost to the victim, of course, is loss of life. This happens in the case of a murder victim.

Costs to Society

In addition to the costs borne by the criminal and the victim of crime, there are addition costs that are borne by society. Some of these costs are as follows:

- Increased taxes   Crime prevention is expensive. Street lights, surveillance cameras, and extra police presence are needed in neighbourhoods with high crime rates. These services have to be financed by higher taxes.
- Reduced property values   As the crime rate increases in a community, the values of properties in that community decrease. Prime residential communities have been known to degenerate into slums because of crimes.

- Loss of freedom   Freedom is something that is highly regarded. We want to be free to take a walk in the evening, sit by the side of a lake, go window shopping in the evening, or ride a bike in a park. Crime may force us to curtail such pleasurable activities and become prisons in our own homes.

- Reduced education and health services   Monies spent on drug rehabilitation, maintaining criminals in penal institutions, various forms of crime prevention, etc. could be used to provide education, health, and other desirable services for the community.

Reasons for Crime

A question well worth asking is this: Why do people commit crimes? Different people will give different answers, some of which may include:

- Because they are hungry
- Because they are covetous
- Because they are wicked
- Because they are greedy
- Because they are on drugs
- Because of emotional issues
- Because they are sinful

Without carrying out a detailed sophisticated analysis of the reasons for crime, we will discuss some of the root causes to give you a better understanding of some of the motives behind criminal activities.

Unemployment

Unemployed people have a great deal of idle time on their hands. At the same time, their need for goods and services persists while their ability to satisfy those needs diminishes because of unemployment. Such people may turn to crime as a means of satisfying their needs.

Poverty

Undoubtedly, poverty is one of the root causes of crime. Since people do not have the financial resources to provide the goods and services they want, they resort to criminal activities which may be an easy way to acquire what they want.

Drugs

People who are under the influence of drugs behave differently from when they are not under the influence. One may become addicted to certain drugs; then he or she be willing to commit whatever crime necessary to obtain the drug.

Peer Pressure

Young people, especially teenagers, are usually influenced by their peers. They look to their peers for validation in terms of how they talk, what they wear, where they hang out, etc. They may be pressured into illegal activities such as gang violence, underage consumption of alcohol, robbery, author theft, and other types of criminal activities.

Failure to obtain Justice

In an unjust society, where some members find it difficult to obtain justice, those members may feel they have no choice but to take the law into their own hands. By so doing, they may actually commit crimes. The acts may be understandable or even *justifiable,* yet criminal.

Back to the Bible

Earlier in this chapter, we looked at some verses in the Bible concerning crime. What does the wisest man say about the issue? Solomon's thoughts are expressed below:

Because the sentence against an evil deed is not executed speedily, the heart of the children of man is fully set to do evil. Though a sinner does evil a hundred times and prolongs his life, yet I know that it will be well with those who fear God, because they fear before him. But it will not be well with the wicked, neither will he prolong his days like a shadow, because he does not fear before God.

There is a vanity that takes place on earth, that there are righteous people to whom it happens according to the deeds of the wicked, and there are wicked people to whom it happens according to the deeds of the righteous. I said that this also is vanity. And I commend joy, for man has nothing better under the sun but to eat and drink and be joyful, for this will go with him in his toil through the days of his life that God has given him under the sun.

When I applied my heart to know wisdom, and to see the business that is done on earth, how neither day nor night do one's eyes see sleep, then I saw all the work of God, that man cannot find out the work that is done under the sun. However much man may toil in seeking, he will not find it out. Even though a wise man claims to know, he cannot find it out. **(Ecclesiastes 8:11-17)**

The main points are that there are no advantages to wickedness, and man cannot find out the work of God.

A Few Tips on Crime Prevention

Many of the steps you can take to prevent crime are common sense in nature. Here are a few of them:

Increase the Cost to the Criminal

Criminals, like other individuals, don't like to incur costs. By making it more difficult for criminals to engage in criminal activities, you are actually increasing the cost of committing crime. In this regard, you can install locks, install burglar bars, remove ladders out of sight, and secure vulnerable doors and windows. You can also remove easily stolen items such as handbags, wallets, purses, keys, laptop computers, and cell phones. Locking the doors to your home, office, and car is an effective way of deterring crime.

Reducing the Profit from Crime

Criminals engage in criminal activities because there are benefits to be derived. For example, they may steal with the intention of selling the stolen items for cash. By reducing the profits that can be derived from such activities, you will reduce the incentive to engage in them. For example, the branding of cattle greatly reduced the pilferage of livestock from the Ponderosa. People will tend to refrain from purchasing items known to be stolen.

Use Lighting Effectively

Accounts suggest that criminals prefer to work in the dark where their actions are hidden. The implication is that proper lighting will deter crime. Lights in and around the home or other property can be programmed to go on at designated times, thus giving the impression that someone is there. The mere fact of lights going on and off is a deterrent.

Maintain your Property

Dilapidated houses and generally slum neighborhoods seem to attract criminals. By maintaining your home in a state of good repair, and ensuring that waste is removed from your surroundings, you will be discouraging criminals.

Report Suspicious Movements

If you see something suspicious or someone wandering about suspiciously, report it to the relevant authorities. This could be a case of crime planning, especially if the individual is not from the neighbourhood.

Do Not Allow Mail to Accumulate

The accumulation of mail in mail boxes can be interpreted as absence from home. This can serve as an invitation for unwanted visitors, including criminals, to enter and commit a crime. Arrange for a family member or friend to pick up your mail if you plan to be away for a few days.

Change Routines

Criminals often look for patterns in the behaviors of their victims. You can throw them off guard by changing your routine. For example, instead of going to the bank religiously on Fridays at 10:00 a.m., you can switch it up by frequently changing the day and the time. You can also frustrate the plans of criminals by regularly changing your route to the bank.

Hope and Crime

Crime is obviously undesirable from the point of view of the victims. Criminals themselves can conceivable benefit from crime prevention. A question well worth asking is this: What does hope have to do with crime? One way of addressing the question is to consider what is likely to happen in the absence of hope. If people abandon hope and adopt the attitude that all is lost as far as the fight against crime is concerned, then they may see no point in taking any measures to prevent crime. They may simply pull up stakes and move on, leaving the neighborhood to the criminals.

The hope of a better life in the future will give us an incentive to practice all the techniques and strategies that will prevent the occurrence of crime. Hope that criminals can be rehabilitated can motivate us to participate in and support crime rehabilitation programs. Finally, hope of a new earth where crime does not exist will enable us to endure all the negative effects of crime until Jesus comes to take us home.

Prayer

Most kind and ever-loving Father, our society is suffering immensely from criminal activities. Your Word tells us that crime proceeds from the heart. So, Father, we pray that you will create in us pure hearts and renew right spirits within us. Help us to love each other so that we can live without fear of crime.

Amen

Pathways to a Brighter Future

CHAPTER 17: HELL

*Hell is a real place prepared for
the devil and his angels*
.

The way of life winds upward for the wise, that he may turn away from hell below. (Proverbs 15:24)

If someone tells you to "Go to hell", whether or not you believe in hell, you know that he or she is not sending you to a land filled with milk and honey. It's a place you'd rather not go. What does "hell on earth" suggest to you? What do you think of an experience described as "pure hell"? Is hell a real place? What is it like? Who are its inhabitants? If you have been pondering over some of *these questions, you are not alone. In this chapter, we provide some answers based on the infallible Word of God.*

What is Hell?

Unfortunately, the word "hell" is used in the Bible to refer to the grave, and also to the place where the wicked will go after the final judgment. Unfortunately, the double meaning has the potential to confuse. In this book, we define hell as the place of punishment, where the devil, his angels, and all evil and sinful people who refuse God's offer of salvation will be sent to be burnt. The Bible describes it as a lake of fire:

And the beast was captured, and with it the false prophet who had performed in its presence the signs by which he deceived those who had received the mark of the beast and those who worshiped its image. These two were thrown alive into the lake of fire that burns with sulfur. **(Revelation 19:20)**

Hell is Real

We have no intention of going to hell so its exact location would serve only curiosity value. We cannot provide geographical location in terms of latitude and longitude. However, we want to verify that it is a real place so that we can avoid it at all costs. Many Bible verses can be used to substantiate the view that hell is a real place, but we will limit ourselves to the following three passages:

But the cowardly, the unbelieving, the vile, the murderers, the sexually immoral, those who practice magic arts, the idolaters and all liars—they will be consigned to the fiery lake of burning sulfur. This is the second death. **(Revelation 21:8)**

Then he will say to those on his left, 'Depart from me, you who are cursed, into the eternal fire prepared for the devil and his angels. **(Matthew 25:41)**

If your hand causes you to stumble, cut it off. It is better for you to enter life maimed than with two hands to go into hell, where the fire never goes out. **(Mark 9:43)**

Clearly, to be consigned to a fiery lake, or to be sent into the eternal fire, or to go into hell where the fire never goes out all suggest a real place. Just as heaven is a real place where the good are rewarded for their good deeds, so too, hell is a real place where the wicked are punished for their evil deeds.

Sayings about Hell

Hell is such an intriguing topic that it would be surprising if there were not many perceptive and insightful quotes about it. Here are some quotes about hell that will provide some good food for thought.

An intelligent hell would be better than a stupid paradise. **Victor Hugo**

Hell is empty and all the devils are here. **William Shakespeare**

Oh, my brothers and sisters in Christ, if sinners will be damned, at least let them leap to hell over our bodies; and if they will perish, let them perish with our arms about their knees, imploring them to stay, and not madly to destroy themselves. If hell must be filled, at least let it be filled in the teeth of our exertions, and let

HOPE

not one go there unwarned and unprayed for. **Charles Spurgeon**

If you're going through hell, keep going. **Winston Churchill**

Hell is the highest reward that the devil can offer you for being a servant of his. **Billy Sunday**

Hell is a place, a time, a consciousness, in which there is no love. **Richard Bach**

Go to Heaven for the climate, Hell for the company. **Mark Twain**

There is no greater hell than to be a prisoner of fear. **Ben Jonson**

Religion is for people who are scared to go to hell. Spirituality is for people who have already been there. **Bonnie Raitt**

The safest road to hell is the gradual one - the gentle slope, soft underfoot, without sudden turnings, without milestones, without signposts. **C. S. Lewis**

I don't like to commit myself about heaven and hell - you see, I have friends in both places. **Mark Twain**

I don't believe in an afterlife, so I don't have to spend my whole life fearing hell, or fearing heaven even more. For whatever the tortures of hell, I think the boredom of heaven would be even worse. **Isaac Asimov**

I hold it to be the inalienable right of anybody to go to hell in his own way. **Robert Frost**

When I pastored a country church, a farmer didn't like the sermons I preached on hell. He said, Preach about the meek and lowly Jesus. I said, That's where I got my information about hell. **Vance Havner**

I think that hell essentially is separation from God forever. And that is the worst hell that I can think of. But I think people have a hard time believing God is going to allow people to burn in literal fire forever. I think the fire that is mentioned in the Bible is a burning thirst for God that can never be quenched. **Billy Graham**

The hell of these days is the fear of not getting along, especially of not making money. **Thomas Carlyle**

Hell is oneself, hell is alone, the other figures in it merely projections. There is nothing to escape from and nothing to escape to. One is always alone. **T. S. Eliot**

Hell isn't merely paved with good intentions; it's walled and roofed with them. Yes, and furnished too. **Aldous Huxley**

The mind is its own place, and in itself, can make heaven of Hell, and a hell of Heaven. **John Milton**

In hell there is no other punishment than to begin over and over again the tasks left unfinished in your lifetime. **Andre Gide**

Source:
https://www.azquotes.com/quotes/topics/hell.html

Bible Verses about Hell

Now that we have paid some attention to what some people have to say about hell, let us see what God's Holy Word has to say. References to hell in the Bible are many. The following is a sample.

HOPE

(If your right eye makes you stumble, tear it out and throw it from you; for it is better for you to lose one of the parts of your body, than for your whole body to be thrown into hell. If your right hand makes you stumble, cut it off and throw it from you; for it is better for you to lose one of the parts of your body, than for your whole body to go into hell. **(Matthew 5:29-30)**

Do not fear those who kill the body but are unable to kill the soul; but rather fear Him who is able to destroy both soul and body in hell. **(Matthew 10:28)**

But I say to you that everyone who is angry with his brother shall be guilty before the court; and whoever says to his brother, 'You good-for-nothing,' shall be guilty before the supreme court; and whoever says, 'You fool,' shall be guilty enough to go into the fiery hell. **(Matthew 5:22)**

And the devil who deceived them was thrown into the lake of fire and brimstone, where the beast and the false prophet are also; and they will be tormented day and night forever and ever. **(Revelation 20:10)**

"Then He will also say to those on His left, 'Depart from Me, accursed ones, into the eternal fire which has been prepared for the devil and his angels; **(Matthew 25:41)**

And the beast was seized, and with him the false prophet who performed the signs in his presence, by which he deceived those who had received the mark of the beast and those who worshiped his image; these two were thrown alive into the lake of fire which burns with brimstone. **(Revelation 19:20)**

For if God did not spare angels when they sinned, but cast them into hell and committed them to pits of darkness, reserved for judgment; **(2 Peter 2:4)**

Pathways to a Brighter Future

You serpents, you brood of vipers, how will you escape the sentence of hell? **(Matthew 23:33)**

And the sea gave up the dead which were in it, and death and Hades gave up the dead which were in them; and they were judged, every one of them according to their deeds. Then death and Hades were thrown into the lake of fire. This is the second death, the lake of fire. And if anyone's name was not found written in the book of life, he was thrown into the lake of fire. **(Revelation 20:13-15)**

The Impact of a Belief in Hell

If people believe that hell is a real place where wicked and sinful people go to face the punishment for their evil deeds, and if they believe that such punishment involves being burnt alive in a fiery lake, it stands to reason that the fear of hell will deter people from living sinful lives. There are those who believe that people should do good not because of fear of burning forever in hell's fire, but because they love God, believe in Jesus Christ, and he asks them to keep his commandments.

Imagine, if you will, a community that has existed for decades without any knowledge of hell. Of course, it has laws and customs forbidding it to commit murder, steal, tell lies, and engage in other criminal activities. A Christian preacher came into the community to conduct an evangelistic crusade. He preached about Satan, sin, and hell and convinced many in the community that in the judgment, those who did not obey God's laws would burn eternally in hell's fire. Such a conviction would likely transform that community. Murder, stealing, sexual immorality, bearing false witness, covetousness, rape, devil worship, and other acts of lawlessness would doubtlessly decrease in that community. The crime rate would fall significantly and so would the cost of crime (See Chapter 16).

The Purpose of Hell

Houseflies are among the most annoying creatures. They are relentless in their perseverance, and they are just plain nasty. When I was a child, I was sure that they served no useful purpose. As I grew older and wiser, I learned that houseflies, yes, those annoying pests, act as scavengers eating rotting organic matter and thus playing an important role in our environment. They consume our rubbish and dead animal carcasses. Moreover, they are used in commercial fish and livestock feed. If we believe in the principle that everything that exists has a purpose, then a legitimate question to ask is, What is the purpose of hell? To answer this question, we will refer to the source of ultimate truth and wisdom, that is, the Word of God.

It is not God's will that any should perish, but that all should come to repentance (2 Peter 2:9). He wants everyone to accept salvation that He offers freely, and live with Him in heaven. He is a kind, loving, and merciful Father, but he is also fair and just. God created us with a free will. Before us we have good and evil. He points out to us the consequences of each course of action and advises us to choose good. If we choose evil, we bear the consequences—hell's fire.

Hell was not intended for us, but for the Devil and his angels. Witness Matthew 25:41:

Then he will say to those on his left, 'Depart from me, you cursed, into the eternal fire prepared for the devil and his angels.

Hell was prepared for the Devil and his angels, but those who reject God's salvation offered through Jesus Christ will join them in hell. The Bible makes this fact abundantly clear:

But as for the cowardly, the faithless, the detestable, as for murderers, the sexually immoral, sorcerers, idolaters, and all liars, their portion will be in the lake that burns with fire and sulfur, which is the second death." **(Revelation 21:8)**

If God really loves us, why does He allow us to go to hell? Some people do not believe that God will allow us to burn in hell. We must remember though, that it is not His will for us to go to hell. It is our choice. His expressed will for us is that:

I go to prepare a place for you. And if I go and prepare a place for you, I will come again and receive you to Myself, that where I am, there you may be also. **(John 14:2-3)**.

Surely, God loves us and wants the best for us.

Hope and Hell

We have seen that hell is a real place where at the final judgment, Satan, his evil angels, and all those who reject God's offer of salvation through Jesus Christ will be thrown into hell's burning fire. No one wants to go to hell, and we don't want ourselves or our loved ones to end up there.

Therefore, we entertain a glimmer of hope that no one we care for ends up there. Hope, that powerful force that resides within the human spirit and prevents us from giving up, keeps us praying and believing that one day, our loved ones will turn away from a life of sin and accept the salvation the is so freely offered and thus avoid hearing those words, "Depart from me ye workers of iniquity." (Matthew 7:23).

No matter how gloomy the situation might be, as long as there is life, hope is the light that flickers in the darkest of times, the belief that the possibility exists for redemption and renewal. Hope serves as a beacon, guiding individuals towards the path of transformation and liberation from the clutches of the enemy of our souls.

If we can inspire hope within individuals who are going down the wrong path, that they can enjoy a better life and enjoy brimstone and fire in hell, it is possible by the grace of God, that they will seek forgiveness and avert ultimate destruction in hell.

Prayer

Almighty God, we are Your children and we know that You love us and that it is not Your will that any of us should perish. We know, dear God, that hell is a real place prepared for the devil and his angels. Father, You have made it possible for us to escape the fires of hell, and we thank you. In the name of Jesus Christ, our Lord and Saviour, we pray that we will accept the salvation that is so freely offered.

Amen

Pathways to a Brighter Future

CHHAPTER 18: GRACE

Out of the fullness of His grace, God has blessed us all.

But because of his great love for us, God, who is rich in mercy, made us alive with Christ even when we were dead in transgressions—it is by grace you have been saved. (Ephesians 2:4-5)

Introduction

I wrote what appeared to be the final chapter of this book when I described the New Earth. Then I thought of the passage of scripture quoted by Paul:

But as it is written, Eye hath not seen, nor ear heard, neither have entered into the heart of man, the things which God hath prepared for them that love him (1 Corinthians 2:9)

I also remembered the city described by John in Revelation 21. It has walls of jasper, it is made of pure gold; its foundation is made of sapphire, emerald, beryl, topaz, and other precious stones. Its gates are made of pearls. In this city, the glory of God gives the light and the Lamb is the lamp.

Then it occurred to me that we can enjoy all this only by *grace*—the grace of God. So I decided to write a chapter on Grace before considering the book finished.

Grace Defined

As a noun, grace is often defined as an undeserved, unearned gift from God. I recall when I was a child, hearing somewhere, either in school or in church, that grace is God's unmerited favour to mankind. Grace is also used to refer to elegance, sophistication, and gentleness in movement. Such is the case when a dancer or gymnast is described as moving with grace. As a verb, grace is used to mean, "bring honour or dignity", as when we say, "We are hoping that she will grace us with her presence at the recital." Here, we use grace as a noun to refer to God's unmerited gift freely bestowed to mankind.

Sayings about Grace

Our understanding of grace and its significance can be widened and deepened by paying attention to what others have to say about it. What follows in this section is a collection of sayings about grace that is designed to help us to consider various views about grace. Some of the sayings are profound while others might elicit a chuckle. Also, different sayings of the same individual may be recorded. We may encounter perspectives that we have not considered before.

"I do not at all understand the mystery of grace - only that it meets us where we are but does not leave us where it found us." **Anne Lamott**

"Grace is the voice that calls us to change and then gives us the power to pull it off." **Max Lucado**

"Our worst days are never so bad that you are beyond the reach of God's grace. And your best days are never so good that you are beyond the need of God's grace." **Jerry Bridges**

"We can be certain that God will give us the strength and resources we need to live through any situation in life that he ordains. The will of God will never take us where the grace of God cannot sustain us." **Billy Graham**

"Believe the best about people. Pray for their short comings. You are not the standard. We all need grace." **LeCrae**

"Grace is a power that comes in and transforms a moment into something better." **Caroline Myss**

"Grant me the grace to dissolve my negative thoughts about myself today. I breathe the grace of kindness into my heart. And may the grace of healing flow abundantly to every one in need of help." **Caroline Myss**

"In the New Testament grace means God's love in action towards men who merited the opposite of love. Grace means God moving heaven and earth to save sinners who could not lift a finger to save themselves." **J. I. Packer**

"The grace of God means something like: Here is your life. You might never have been, but you are because the party wouldn't have been complete without you." **Frederick Buechner**

"Grace is the overflowing favor of God, and you can always count on it being available to draw upon as needed." **Oswald Chambers**

"Grace is the outcome of inward harmony." **Marie von Ebner-Eschenbach**

"Courage is grace under pressure." **Ernest Hemingway**

"God answers the mess of life with one word: Grace." **Max Lucado**

"Faith is a living, daring, confidence in God's grace." **Martin Luther**

"Grace is ever present. All that is necessary is that you surrender to it." **Ramana Maharshi**

"We need to remember that we are saved by grace when we fail. But we need to remember it much more when we succeed." **Timothy Keller**

"Love cannot be learned or taught. Love comes as Grace." **Rumi**

"Man is born broken. He lives by mending. The Grace of God is glue." **Eugene O'Neill**

"A man is not saved against his will, but he is made willing by the operation of the Holy Ghost. A mighty grace which he does not wish to resist enters into the man, disarms him, makes a new creature of him, and he is saved. **Charles Spurgeon**

Soar back through all your own experiences. Think of how the Lord has led you in the wilderness and has fed and clothed you every day. How God has borne with your ill manners, and put up with all your murmurings and all your longings after the 'sensual pleasures of Egypt!' Think of how the Lord's grace has been sufficient for you in all your troubles. **Charles Spurgeon**

Source: https://www.azquotes.com/quotes/topics/grace.html

The Bible on Grace

In the previous section, some people have shared their views on grace with us. So we have a fairly wide spectrum of ideas on grace. We now turn our attention to what the Bible has to say about grace. It should not be surprising that grace is mentioned 170 times in the King James Version of the Bible in the Old and New Testaments. We have no intention to list all Biblical references to grace, but we will list a fair sample to give you, the reader, a good idea of what the Bible has to say about grace.

For the Lord your God is gracious and compassionate. He will not turn his face from you if you return to him. **(2 Chronicles 30:9)**

But in your great mercy you did not put an end to them or abandon them, for you are a gracious and merciful God. **(Nehemiah 9:31)**

HOPE

Yet the Lord longs to be gracious to you; therefore he will rise up to show you compassion. For the Lord is a God of justice. Blessed are all who wait for him! **(Isaiah 30:18)**

Out of the fullness of his grace he has blessed us all, giving us one blessing after another. God gave the Law through Moses, but grace and truth came through Jesus Christ. **(John 1:16-17)**

For all have sinned and fall short of the glory of God, and are justified by his grace as a gift, through the redemption that is in Christ Jesus, whom God put forward as a propitiation by his blood, to be received by faith. This was to show God's righteousness, because in his divine forbearance he had passed over former sins. **(Romans 3:23-25)**

Therefore, since we have been justified by faith, we have peace with God through our Lord Jesus Christ. Through him we have also obtained access by faith into this grace in which we stand, and we rejoice in hope of the glory of God. **(Romans 5:1-2)**

So too at the present time there is a remnant, chosen by grace. But if it is by grace, it is no longer on the basis of works; otherwise grace would no longer be grace. **(Romans 11:5-6)**

For by grace you have been saved through faith. And this is not your own doing; it is the gift of God, not a result of works, so that no one may boast. **(Ephesians 2:8-9)**

Therefore do not be ashamed of the testimony about our Lord, nor of me his prisoner, but share in suffering for the gospel by the power of God, who saved us and called us to a holy calling, not because of our works but because of his own purpose and grace, which he gave us in Christ Jesus before the ages began, and which now has been manifested through the appearing of our Savior Christ Jesus, who abolished death and brought life and immortality to light through the gospel. **(2 Timothy 1:8-10)**

He saved us, not because of works done by us in righteousness, but according to his own mercy, by the washing of regeneration and renewal of the Holy Spirit, whom he poured out on us richly through Jesus Christ our Savior, so that being justified by his grace we might become heirs according to the hope of eternal life. **(Titus 3:5-7)**

For sin will have no dominion over you, since you are not under law but under grace. **(Romans 6:14)**

But by the grace of God I am what I am, and his grace toward me was not in vain. On the contrary, I worked harder than any of them, though it was not I, but the grace of God that is with me. **(1 Corinthians 15:10)**

And God is able to make all grace abound to you, so that having all sufficiency in all things at all times, you may abound in every good work. **(2 Corinthians 9:8)**

But he said to me, "My grace is sufficient for you, for my power is made perfect in weakness." Therefore I will boast all the more gladly of my weaknesses, so that the power of Christ may rest upon me. **(2 Corinthians 12:9)**

You then, my child, be strengthened by the grace that is in Christ Jesus, and what you have heard from me in the presence of many witnesses entrust to faithful men, who will be able to teach others also. **(2 Timothy 2:1-2)**

For the grace of God has appeared, bringing salvation for all people, training us to renounce ungodliness and worldly passions, and to live self-controlled, upright, and godly lives in the present age, waiting for our blessed hope, the appearing of the glory of our great God and Savior Jesus Christ, who gave himself for us to redeem us from all lawlessness and to purify for himself a people for his own possession who are zealous for good works. **(Titus 2:11-14)**

Let us then with confidence draw near to the throne of grace, that we may receive mercy and find grace to help in time of need. **(Hebrews 4:16)**

But he gives more grace. Therefore it says, "God opposes the proud but gives grace to the humble." **(James 4:6)**

As each has received a gift, use it to serve one another, as good stewards of God's varied grace: whoever speaks, as one who speaks oracles of God; whoever serves, as one who serves by the strength that God supplies—in order that in everything God may be glorified through Jesus Christ. To him belong glory and dominion forever and ever. Amen. **(1 Peter 4:10-11)**

Source: https://www.biblelyfe.com/blog/bible-verses-about-grace

What can we learn from the above passages of scripture about grace? Among other things, we can learn the following:

1. We are justified (made right) by the gift of grace.

2. We are chosen by grace, not by work.

3. We are saved by grace through faith.

4. God gave us grace through Jesus Christ before the the beginning of the ages.

5. It is through grace that we become heirs of eternal life.

6. We are not under law but under grace.

7. God's grace is sufficient for us.

The Significance of Grace

Grace is a concept that holds immense significance in the human experience, transcending cultural and denominational boundaries. Whether you are Catholic, Moravian, Methodist, Anglican, Seventh-day Adventist, Pentecostal, or other, you have some notion that grace is something good that comes from God. Even those of you who may not be religious recognize grace as something good. At its core, grace represents a quality of elegance, poise, and benevolence that elevates our interactions with others and ourselves. It embodies the ability to exhibit kindness, compassion, and forgiveness, even in the face of adversity. The importance of grace in our everyday lives lies in its power to transform relationships, foster understanding, and promote a harmonious existence.

In our interactions with others, grace serves as a potent force for building bridges and mending broken connections. When we approach conflicts and disagreements with grace, we cultivate an atmosphere of empathy and respect. It allows us to recognize the inherent humanity in others, even when their actions may be hurtful or misguided. By extending grace to those around us, we create an environment where misunderstandings can be resolved, and genuine understanding can take root.

Furthermore, grace plays a vital role in self-growth and personal development. Embracing grace towards oneself involves accepting imperfections and mistakes with a compassionate heart. Instead of dwelling on failures, grace encourages us to learn from them and move forward with newfound wisdom. Through self-grace, we foster resilience, self-compassion, and a positive sense of self-worth, all of which are vital for mental and emotional well-being.

Spiritually, grace often finds its place as a divine force that offers unmerited blessings and redemption. In various religious traditions, grace represents the boundless love and forgiveness of a higher power, which empowers individuals to seek transformation and find solace in times of despair. This notion of divine grace inspires many to strive for acts of kindness and charity, extending its impact beyond personal relationships to benefit communities and societies.

In a world often marked by haste and harshness, the importance of grace cannot be overstated. It reminds us to slow down, reflect, and choose compassion over judgment. Grace encourages us to see the best in others and to treat them with the same kindness we wish to receive. By embracing grace in our lives, we pave the way for understanding, healing, and a more interconnected and harmonious world.

The following fictitious story emphasizes the significance of grace in our lives. Pete is considered the village drunk. In the mornings, he crawls out of his shed made of galvanized iron and cardboard, makes his way to the village dump, and searches for scraps of food and other discarded items. His clothes can be described accurately as "dirty rags" and his "shoes" are tied onto his feet by old strings. On one occasion, a man was seen

Pathways to a Brighter Future

looking at Pete, shaking his head and saying softly, "There go I but for the grace of God."

But for the grace of God, what would I be? What would you be?

The songwriter expressed it well when she wrote the following song:

Marvelous Grace

1. Marvelous Grace Of Our Loving Lord,
   Grace That Exceeds Our Sin And Our Guilt!
   Yonder On Calvary's Mount Outpoured,
   There Where The Blood Of The Lamb Was Spilled.
   Chorus

2. Grace, Grace, God's Grace,
   Grace That Will Pardon And Cleanse Within;
   Grace, Grace, God's Grace,
   Grace That Is Greater Than All Our Sin!

3. Sin And Despair, Like The Sea Waves Cold,
   Threaten The Soul With Infinite Loss;
   Grace That Is Greater, Yes, Grace Untold,
   Points To The Refuge, The Mighty Cross.

4. Marvelous, Infinite, Matchless Grace,
   Freely Bestowed On All Who Believe!
   You That Are Longing To See His Face,
   Will You This Moment His Grace Receive? **Julia H. Johnston**

When we pause to consider the wonderful gift of salvation through the grace of God, we can hardly resist the urge to join John Newton in singing

HOPE

Amazing Grace

Amazing grace how sweet the sound
That saved a wretch like me
I once was lost, but now I'm found
Was blind but now I see

'Twas grace that taught my heart to fear
And grace my fears relieved
How precious did that grace appear
The hour I first believed

Through many dangers, toils, and snares
I have already come
This grace that brought me safe thus far
And grace will lead me home

When we've been here ten thousand years
Bright, shining as the sun
We've no less days to sing God's praise
Than when we first begun
John Newton

Indeed, God's grace is nothing short of amazing, and we can be its recipients.

Hope and Grace

In an earlier chapter, we outlined the close relationship that exists between faith and hope. A close relationship also exists between hope and grace. It is grace that gives us the courage to hope. The relationship between these two concepts is one of profound significance, involving two potent and transformative elements of the human experience. Hope, with its untiring optimism and belief in the possibility of positive outcomes, serves as a beacon through life's darkest moments. It is the fuel that powers our resolve, inspiring us to persevere and strive for better circumstances even when situations appear bleak and gloomy.

Grace, on the other hand, is the epiphany of compassion, forgiveness, and acceptance. It is the gentle touch that soothes wounds, both visible and hidden, and enables us to find peace and calmness in the face of turmoil and adversity. When hope and grace converge, a harmonious chemistry emerges. Acts of grace quicken the hope that is within us and energize us to extend kindness, understanding, and tolerance to others. In turn, grace infuses life into hope, granting it the resilience to endure the trials and tribulations of life's unpredictable journey. Together, hope and grace nurture resilience, elevate the human spirit, and illuminate the path toward a more compassionate and promising future.

Prayer

Merciful Father, our King of kings and Lord of lords, we thank You for Your everlasting love and Your amazing grace. Your love is new every morning, and Your grace is immeasurable. We pray, Father, that by Your grace, we will be victorious over sin and Satan.

Amen

HOPE

CHAPTER 19: THE NEW EARTH

Eye hath not seen, nor ear heard, Neither have entered into the heart of man, The things which God hath prepared for them that love him. **(1 Corinthians 2:9)**

"For behold, I create new heavens and a new earth; And the former things will not be remembered or come to mind." **(Isaiah 65:17)**

The Earth God Created

When God created the earth, it was a beautiful place. The light, the sky, land, seas, vegetation, sun, moon, stars, birds, livestock, wild animals, and man were declared by God to be very good. It was our Eden home. A description of this home is important because it gives us an idea of what we have lost because of sin, and what will be restored when Christ returns. This home had many beautiful trees, some of which bore edible fruits.

The **LORD** *God made all kinds of trees grow out of the ground—trees that were pleasing to the eye and good for food. In the middle of the garden were the tree of life and the tree of the knowledge of good and evil.* **(Genesis 2:9)**

The garden was watered by four rivers. These rivers are described in Genesis 2:10-14 as follows:

A river watering the garden flowed from Eden; from there it was separated into four headwaters. The name of the first is the Pishon; it winds through the entire land of Havilah, where there is gold. (The gold of that land is good; aromatic resin and onyx are also there.) The name of the second river is the Gihon; it winds through the entire land of Cush. The name of the third river is the Tigris; it runs along the east side of Ashur. And the fourth river is the Euphrates.

From all accounts, this was the perfect home for mankind. Adam and Eve were free to move about in the beautiful garden and to eat of all the fruits except one. They had the opportunity to fellowship with the Creator and to commune with Him. A heaven on earth? Perhaps!

The Cursed Earth

Adam and Eve disobeyed God and as a consequence, the earth was cursed. First, the serpent was cursed.

So the LORD *God said to the serpent, "Because you have done this, "Cursed are you above all livestock and all wild animals! You will crawl on your belly and you will eat dust all the days of your life.* **(Genesis 3:14)**

Second, the woman, Eve, was cursed. Childbearing would be painful, and she would be subservient to her husband.

To the woman he said, "I will make your pains in childbearing very severe; with painful labor you will give birth to children. Your desire will be for your husband, and he will rule over you." **(Genesis 3:16)**

Third, Adam and the ground were cursed. The tilling of the soil would be laborious and painful, the earth would produce thorns and thistles, and Adam would eat by doing hard physical work.

To Adam he said, "Cursed is the ground because of you; through painful toil you will eat food from it all the days of your life. It will produce thorns and thistles for you, and you will eat the plants of the field. By the sweat of your brow you will eat your food until you return to the ground, since from it you were taken; for dust you are and to dust you will return." **(Genesis 3:17-19)**

Vacation in Heaven

Christ will return to this earth as King Jesus, as he has promised. In John 14:3 He said:

And if I go and prepare a place for you, I will come back and take you to be with me that you also may be where I am.

In Acts 1:10-11, referring to Jesus we read:

And while they were gazing into heaven as he went, behold, two men stood by them in white robes, and said, "Men of Galilee, why do you stand looking into heaven? This Jesus, who was taken up from you into heaven, will come in the same way as you saw him go into heaven."

Not only will Jesus return to earth, but He will also take the saints to heaven with Him. Listen to what the apostle Paul had to say:

"For the Lord Himself will come down from heaven, with a loud command, with the voice of the archangel and with the trumpet call of God, and the dead in Christ will rise first. After that, we who are still alive and are left will be caught up with them in the clouds to meet the Lord in the air. And so we will be with the Lord forever." **(1Thessalonians 4:16-17)**

So the Lord descends from heaven, the righteous dead are resurrected, and with the living saints, they are taken to heaven for 1,000 years (the Millennium). That will be a vacation in heaven. The following poem describes our vacation in heaven.

When I Take My Vacation in Heaven

Here So Many Are Taking Vacation,
To The Mountains, The Lakes Or The Sea;
Where They Rest From Their Cares And Their Worries,
What A Wonderful Time That Must Be!

But It Seems Not My Lot To Be Like Them,
I Must Toil Thru The Heat And The Cold,
Seeking Out The Lost Sheep On The Mountains,
Bringing Wanderers Back To The Fold.

When I Take My Vacation In Heaven,
What A Wonderful Time That Will Be;
Hearing Concerts By The Heavenly
And The Face Of My Saviour I'll See;

HOPE

Sitting Down By The Banks Of The River;
'Neath The Shade Of The Ever Green Tree,
I Shall Rest From My Burdens Forever,
Won't You Spend Your Vacation With Me.

Now Some Day I Shall Take My Vacation
To The City John Tells Us About;
With Its Foundation Walls All So Precious,
Where From Gladness Of Heart I Shall Shout!

O No Sights Ever Witnessed By Mortals,
Can Compare With The Glories Up There
I Shall Spend My Vacation With Jesus,
In The Place He Went On To Prepare.

There The Weather Will Always Be Perfect.
Not A Cloud Shall Sweep Over The Sky;
And No Earthquakes Or Cyclones Shall Threaten,
In The Land Of The "Sweet By And By";

Soon There's Going To Be An Excursion,
I Am Booked For A Ride In The Air.
You're Invited To Share My Vacation,
And The Feast With Our Bridegroom To Share.

Here On Earth When We Take Our Vacation,
We Return To Our Homes By And By;
When I Take My Vacation In Heaven,
In Those Mansions Of Gold In The Sky.

I Shall Dwell With My Saviour Forever,
With Him Sit On His Heavenly Throne;
All The Days Will Be One, Long Vacation,
When My Saviour Takes Me To His Home.
(Herbert Wesley Buffum)

Millennium on Earth

While the saints are on vacation in heaven with the Lord, what is happening on earth? The Devil and his army of evil angels and followers remain on earth. The unrighteous dead bodies that are in their graves remain there. The following vivid description of the earth at that time is given in the Bible:

"And there were noises and thunderings and lightnings; and there was a great earthquake, such a mighty and great earthquake as had not occurred since men were on the earth. Now the great city was divided into three parts, and the cities of the nations fell. And great Babylon was remembered before God, to give her the cup of the wine of the fierceness of His wrath. Then every island fled away, and the mountains were not found. And great hail from Heaven fell upon men, each hailstone about the weight of a talent" **(Revelation 16:18-21)**

This sounds to me like an absolutely desolate place. There is little wonder that it is described in Revelation 20:1 as the *bottomless pit*. This will be the home of the Devil for 1,000 years. He will be bound because he will have no one to deceive. The saints are already on vacation in heaven with conquering King Jesus. The earth then will be a prison for Satan, that old dragon.

"And I saw an angel coming down out of heaven, having the key to the Abyss and holding in his hand a great chain. He seized the dragon, that ancient serpent, who is the devil, or Satan, and bound him for a thousand years. He threw him in the Abyss, and locked and sealed it over him, to keep him from deceiving the nations any more until the thousand years were ended. After that, he must be set free for a short time." **(Revelation 20:1-3)**

The Earth Made New

After the millennium in heaven, the holy city of God will descend from heaven. The wicked dead will be resurrected, and they join Satan's army which is described as numerous as sand on the seashore. They attempt to take the holy city, but God destroyed them with fire. Here is the Bible text:

"But fire came down from heaven and devoured them." **(Revelation 20:9)**

The new earth is our final home. It has been referred to as Eden restored. It is described as follows:

Then I saw "a new heaven and a new earth," for the first heaven and the first earth had passed away, and there was no longer any sea. I saw the Holy City, the new Jerusalem, coming down out of heaven from God, prepared as a bride beautifully dressed for her husband. And I heard a loud voice from the throne saying, "Look! God's dwelling place is now among the people, and he will dwell with them. They will be his people, and God himself will be with them and be their God. 'He will wipe every tear from their eyes. There will be no more death' or mourning or crying or pain, for the old order of things has passed away." **(Revelation 21:1-4)**

Do you remember the rivers that watered the original Garden of Eden? Well, there is also a river in the earth made new. It is called the River of Life. Its water is crystal clear and it originates from the throne of God. In this earth made new, there is the tree of life whose leaves are for the healing of the nations. The curse of the original earth will be removed from our new Edenic home. Other characteristics of the new earth can be gleaned from the following passage:

Pathways to a Brighter Future

Then the angel showed me the river of the water of life, as clear as crystal, flowing from the throne of God and of the Lamb down the middle of the great street of the city. On each side of the river stood the tree of life, bearing twelve crops of fruit, yielding its fruit every month. And the leaves of the tree are for the healing of the nations. No longer will there be any curse. The throne of God and of the Lamb will be in the city, and his servants will serve him. They will see his face, and his name will be on their foreheads. There will be no more night. They will not need the light of a lamp or the light of the sun, for the Lord God will give them light. And they will reign for ever and ever. **(Revelation 22:1-5)**

The characteristics of the new earth are encapsulated in the following verses:

The Pearly White City

There's a holy and beautiful city
Whose builder and ruler is God;
John saw it descending from Heaven,
When Patmos, in exile, he trod;
Its high, massive walls are of jasper,
The city itself is pure gold;
And when my frail tent here is folded,
Mine eyes shall its glory behold.

No heartaches are known in that city,
No teardrops to dampen the eye;
In Heaven, there's no disappointment,
No storm clouds to darken the sky;
The saints that inhabit the mansions
Will live in contentment of theirs.
Thank God I'm bound for that city
And some day its blessings I'll share.

HOPE

In that bright city, pearly white city,
I have a mansion, a harp, and a crown;
Now I am watching, waiting, and longing,
For the white city that's soon coming down.
(Arthur F. Ingler)

Source: https://lyricstranslate.com

I want to be a citizen and a resident of that city. Don't you?

Hope and the New Earth

Through sin, we lost our Eden home. We have hope that through Jesus Christ, sin, Satan, and everything evil will be destroyed. God's people live with the blessed assurance that they will spend 1,000 years in heaven with King Jesus.

We feel sorrow at the death of our loved ones, but the hope of the resurrection of the dead helps us not to grieve as those who have no hope. The hope of a new purified earth where righteousness dwells enables us to withstand trials and tribulations. We are comforted by the prospect of everlasting life in our new Edenic home.

Prayer

Heavenly Father, Jesus has gone to prepare a place for us so that we can be with Him. It is our fervent prayer that we hear those words, "Well done thou good and faithful servant, enter thou into the joy of thy Lord."

Amen

CLOSING REMARKS

One of the objectives of *Hope: Pathways to a Brighter Future,* is to point readers to a path that leads to everlasting life with Jesus our Lord and Saviour. We have embarked on a remarkable journey of faith, and I am impressed to offer a few words of encouragement and support. The journey to our destination—our new Edenic home, has some roses and daisies in the form of victories, moments of elation, and contentment; but it is also strewn with thorns and thistles—trials, tribulations, and moments of bewilderment. In those moments of confusion, perplexities, and gloom, when we feel totally defeated and broken, let us remember that there is absolutely nothing that the omnipotent, omnipresent, and omniscient God cannot fix. All things are possible with God.

The enemy, that old Serpent, the Devil, will try to dissuade us, but let us not fall prey to his wiles. In times of despair, have faith that God can sustain us by His infinite grace. When the road ahead seems steep and rocky, take solace in the knowledge that God's strength is made perfect in our weakness (2 Corinthians 12:9). He is our ever-present help, a refuge in times of trouble, and a constant source of comfort (Psalm 46:1).

Remember that on this journey, you are not alone. There is a community of faith consisting of people who are looking and working towards a better life now and in the future. They may be organized into churches, and other social groups to improve the human condition. If possible, align yourself with one of these groups where you can make your contribution.

HOPE

I beseech you, dear reader, to study the word of God as recorded in the Holy Bible. Let us lift up our heads because our conquering King Jesus is riding on to victory.

I hope that the following lyrics will cheer us up along the way:

How Cheering is the Christian's Hope

1. How cheering is the Christian's hope,
   While toiling here below!
   It bouys us up while this passing through
   This wilderness of woe.

2. It points us to a land of rest,
   Where saints with Christ will reign;
   Where we shall meet the loved of earth,
   And never part again.

3. Fly, lingering moments, fly, O, fly,
   Dear Savior, quickly come!
   We long to see Thee as Thou art,
   And reach that blissful home. **Anonymous**

"Finally, be strong in the Lord and in his mighty power. Put on the full armor of God, so that you can take your stand against the devil's schemes. For our struggle is not against flesh and blood, but against the rulers, against the authorities, against the powers of this dark world and against the spiritual forces of evil in the heavenly realms. Therefore put on the full armor of God, so that when the day of evil comes, you may be able to stand your ground, and after you have done everything, to stand. Stand firm then, with the belt of truth buckled around your waist, with the breastplate of righteousness in place, and with your feet fitted with the readiness that comes from the gospel of peace. In

addition to all this, take up the shield of faith, with which you can extinguish all the flaming arrows of the evil one. Take the helmet of salvation and the sword of the Spirit, which is the word of God.

And pray in the Spirit on all occasions with all kinds of prayers and requests. With this in mind, be alert and always keep on praying for all the Lord's people." (Ephesians 6:10-18)

Readers, it has been a pleasure to be with you on this journey. It seems fitting to end with a verse and chorus of that well-known hymn, We're Marching to Zion.

We're Marching to Zion

Then let our songs abound,
And ev'ry tear be dry;
We're marching through Immanuel's ground,
We're marching through Immanuel's ground
To fairer worlds on high,
To fairer worlds on high.

Chorus

We're marching to Zion,
Beautiful, beautiful, Zion:
We're marching upward to Zion,
The beautiful city of God.

www.ingramcontent.com/pod-product-compliance
Lightning Source LLC
Chambersburg PA
CBHW072152070526
44585CB00015B/1106